1

TABLE OF CONTENTS

DAY TRADING

Master the techniques of trading psychology and manage risk with the complete guide to day trading

Jason H. Collins

DAY TRADING

Ultimate Guide With Strategies & Techniques for Beginners. Become a Successful Trader With Penny Stocks, Option, Forex and Swing Trade in No Time for Making a Living.

(Updated Version)

INTRODUCTION

Day trading, as the name implies, is when you buy and sell financial investments during the day and clear your outstanding trades before you close the market. The primary objective is to make quick profits from any price increase or decrease that happens on a single trading day.

When the stock market opens, any news that is released later on may carry the opening price of a financial instrument on the next trading day. From a strategic point of view, day trading reduces the risk of incurring losses overnight due to differences between the opening price and the closing price of the previous day. Stocks, shares, futures, and currencies are the most actively traded financial instruments of the day.

The most vital issue that a student has to comprehend day commercialism is that whereas it may be profitable, it is also terribly risky. Current statistics show that 70-90 percent of all-day traders suffer losses in their businesses. Such numbers are almost as high as those associated with gambling losses and are a clear indication that day trading is not intended for amateurs who are trying to " Get it big "in a short time. Honestly, there are very few individual investors who have space, cash, or temperament to cope with day-to-day trading losses.

If you're seriously thinking about becoming a day trader, here's some necessary advice about the profession that might benefit you: the funds you need. According to U.S. law, you will need at least $25,000 per day of trade (more than 8 round trips in a single calendar week). You only would like several hundred USD to alter your currency nowadays. Because of the lower start-up investment cost, it might be wise to start investing in currencies if you're a beginner. For comparison, selling coins is also a lot simpler than trading stocks, as you only have a set amount of money that you can choose to sell.

You are sustaining the deficit. Many new-day investors would suffer terrible losses in their first few months. That's how many of them are going to give up before they even start making money. If you start trading on a day, make sure you only use the cash that you can lose. It's a terrible idea to use the money you need for stuff like your mortgage payments, your life insurance plan, and your daily living expenses.

Reduce the risks. One of the biggest causes of day traders losing money is because they don't know how to reduce their losses. There is no specific formula for when and how to minimize the defeats, but maybe this example will help you understand what usually happens. An unskilled day trader buys a stock, and the stock price inevitably begins to fall. The day the dealer wants to hesitate because he is sure that the market will come back soon. The stock price continues to fall during the day, and the day the dealer kicks himself for not having cut his losses sooner. At the closing time of the auction, he tells himself that he has no choice but to hang on to the stock. In the night, negative news is coming out about the stock, making the opening price of the capital, even more, spiraling down. Today, the dealer is much less wealthy than he would have been had he cut his losses when the price first started to fall.

Day trading isn't the same thing as buying. Day traders do not invest their money in financial instruments, at least not in the classical sense. We usually check the prices of shares that are going up or down. A goal is to ride the wave and to secure a place before the movement begins to move the other direction. You don't spend money on a business unless you know that it will deliver quality Day trading is not a sport. Smart day traders sit down on their laptops all day and wait for any price movements. Nothing is soothing or fun about watching price fluctuations and ticker quotes. If you don't have time with this, it's probably better to find another way to make extra money.

CHAPTER 1
What is Day Trading?

Day trading is the buying and selling of securities in one single trading day. This can occur in any type of marketplace that you choose but it is most common in the stock market and in the forex market.

Day trading is very fast paced. You will purchase a stock, bond, option or other security at some point during the day. Then, sometime during the same day, you will sell the security. If you watched the market properly and the trade goes well, you will make a profit from that sale. If you made a mistake with your calculations, you will lose money.

Day trading is a strategy of trading financial securities, such as stocks and currencies, where positions are taken and closed within the same day. Also called short trading, it involves buying a financial security and selling them before the trading day closes.

How short can day trading last? It can be as short as buying and selling in a few minutes, or even seconds! The point is to end the trading day with a square position, i.e., neither long nor short on any financial security.

It doesn't matter how many trades you do during the day. You can trade just once a day or 10 times a day...it doesn't matter. The defining characteristic of day trading is ending the day with a square position.

Day trading can take place in any market, but the most common ones are the stock market and foreign exchange or forex markets.

When you start day trading, you'll need to start looking at financial securities from a different vantage point. For example, if you're used to swing trading or a buy-and-hold approach to stock market investing, you'll need to look at stocks differently when you day trade if you want to profit from it.

Instead of having a longer-term perspective on stocks, you'll need to reorient it to a very short-term one. In particular, you should shift your focus from a company's possible growth over the long term to its possible immediate price actions during the day.

Another area where you'll need to reorient your thinking are gains. Instead of looking at substantial gains, e.g., 10% or more, you'll need to scale down. Given the short time frame, you may have to make do with gains as low as 1% to 2%. This is because day trading involves trading at a higher frequency but with smaller gains, which accumulate over time.

You do not want to let your trade go on to the next day. This requires a different type of strategy than you will use with day trading. Mixing strategies during the same trade just to avoid a loss will actually make things worse. It is better to cut your losses with that trade and move on, closing out the trade before the end of the day.

11

With day trading, you are not going to make a ton of money off each trade. In fact, if you make a few dollars with each trade, you are doing a good job. The point here is to do a lot of little trades, taking advantage of the temporary ups and downs of the market. A lot of little profits can add up to a good payday when the process is done.

The potential profit that you can make from day traded is often misunderstood on Wall Street. There are many internet scams that like to take on this confusion and capitalize on it making a ton of money by promising large returns in a short period of time. On the other side, the media continues to promote this trading method as a get rich quick scheme.

To determine whether you will be successful depends on a few important factors. Mainly, if you jump into the day trading game without enough knowledge about the market and how this trading method works, you will probably fail. But there are many day traders who are able to make a successful living from day trading. These individuals know about the market, have a good strategy in place, and can work with the market, despite the risks.

Day trading can be difficult. There are many professional financial advisors and money managers who worry about the risk of day trading and will shy away from it. They worry that in many cases, the reward is not going to justify all the risk that you take with day trading. It is possible to make a profit in this method but you have to really know the market and you must have the time to fully watch the market at all times while completing your trade. Even those who do well in day trading will admit that the success rate with this method is often lower than the other methods of stock market trading.

Day trading isn't just restricted to stocks. You can day trade currencies, you can day trade commodities as well as options. Day trading involves more of a set of practices that you stick to.

Day trading is the very definition of short term trading. It's all about the short term. In fact, your trading horizon is restricted to one day. This means that you open a position and you close it strictly within one day's trading hours. You engage in it daily, you focus on one or more stocks or one or more commodities or currency pairings or options.

It's important to keep in mind that all your positions are liquidated by the end of the day. Whether you make money or not, you are out of your position by the end of the day. That is the key definition of day trading.

How Day Trading Decisions Are Made

A day trader's decision whether to enter a stock or exit a stock all boils down to the probable movement of the pricing of the stock within the trading period. The trading period can be as short as 5 minutes or less or it can be the whole day. Whatever the case may be, it doesn't exceed the whole day.

Day traders make money off volatility. They do not make as much money when the stock is trading sideways for a long time and gradually slopes up. A stock might gain value 10% over the course of a year, but that stock, for all intents and purposes, is off limits to a day trader because the volatility isn't there. They would rather trade a stock that bounces 15% up and down, every single day. That stock has enough internal volatility on a day to day basis for day traders to make quite a bit of money.

What Benefit Do Day Traders Offer to the Market?

In terms of economic benefits, how does day trading benefit stock trading as a whole? Well, if anything, day traders provide liquidity to the stock market. They offer a ready base of buyers and sellers of stock. This provides the necessary movement of a stock's price that may encourage other traders to look at either the short term or long-term value and prospects of the stock. In other words, by providing action on a strictly short-term basis, day traders tend to shine a light on the overall attractiveness of a stock.

Keep in mind this is quite ironic because day traders, as a rule, do not look at the fundamentals of a stock. They don't look at the price/earnings ratio or P/E. They don't look at long term value, they don't look at industry positioning. They couldn't care less about any of that. Instead, they focus more on momentum, share movement, share volume and price velocity going either up or down.

How Day Trading Works

Once you start day trading, you can use a myriad number of techniques and methods to execute trades. For example, you can choose to trade based solely on your "gut feeling" or you can go to the other extreme of relying entirely on mathematical models that optimize trading success through elaborate automated trading systems.

Regardless of the method, you can have limitless day-trading profit potential once you master day trading. Here are some of the strategies many expert day traders use profitably.

One is what's called "trading the news", which is one of the most popular day trading strategies since time immemorial. As you may have already gleaned from the name, it involves acting upon any press-released information such as economic data, interest rates, and corporate earnings.

Another popular day trading strategy is called "fading the gap at the open". This one's applicable on trading days when a security's price opens with a gap, i.e., below the previous day's lowest price or above the previous day's highest price. "Fading the gap at the open" means taking an opposite position from the gap's direction. If the price opens with a downward gap, i.e., below the previous day's lowest price, you buy the security. If the price opens with an upward gap, i.e., it opens higher than the previous day's highest price, you short or sell the security.

There was a time when the only people able to trade in financial markets were those working for trading houses, brokerages, and financial institutions. The rise of the internet, however, made things easier for individual traders to get in on the action. Day Trading, in particular, can be a very profitable career, as long as one goes about it in the right way.

However, it can be quite challenging for new traders, especially those who lack a good strategy. Furthermore, even the most experienced day traders hit rough patches occasionally. As stated earlier, Day Trading is the purchase and sale of an asset within a single trading day. It can happen in any marketplace, but it is more common in the stock and forex markets.

Day traders use short-term trading strategies and a high level of leverage to take advantage of small price movements in highly liquid currencies or stocks. Experienced day traders have their finger on events that lead to short-term price movements, such as the news, corporate earnings, economic statistics, and interest rates, which are subject to market psychology and market expectations. When the market exceeds or fails to meet those expectations, it causes unexpected, significant moves that can benefit attuned day traders. However, venturing into this line of business is not a decision prospective day trader should take lightly. It is possible for day traders to make a comfortable living trading for a few hours each day.

However, for new traders, this kind of success takes time. Think like several months or more than a year. For most day traders, the first year is quite tough. It is full of numerous wins and losses, which can stretch anyone's nerves to the limit. Therefore, a day trader's first realistic goal should be to hold on to his/her trading capital.

Volatility is the name of the game when it comes to Day Trading. Traders rely on a market or stock's fluctuations to make money. They prefer stocks that bounce around several times a day, but do not care about the reason for those price fluctuations. Day traders will also go for stocks with high liquidity, which will allow them to enter and exit positions without affecting the price of the stock.

Day traders might short sell a stock if its price is decreasing or purchase if it is increasing. Actually, they might trade it several times in a day, purchasing it and short-selling it a number of times, based on the changing market sentiment. In spite of the trading strategy used, their wish is for the stock price to move.

Day Trading, however, is tricky for two main reasons. Firstly, day traders often compete with professionals, and secondly, they tend to have psychological biases that complicate the trading process.

Professional day traders understand the traps and tricks of this form of trading. In addition, they leverage personal connections, trading data subscriptions, and state-of-the-art technology to succeed. However, they still make losing trades.

Some of these professionals are high-frequency traders whose aim is to skim pennies off every trade.

The Day Trading field is a crowded playground, which is why professional day traders love the participation of inexperienced traders. Essentially, it helps them make more money. In addition, retail traders tend to hold on to losing trades too long and sell winning trades too early.

Due to the urge to close a profitable trade to make some money, retail investors sort of pick the flowers and water the weeds. In other words, they have a strong aversion to making even a small loss. This tends to tie their hands behind their backs when it comes to purchasing a declining asset. This is due to the fear that it might decline further.

CHAPTER 2
Dos and Don'ts of Day Trading

Dos of day trading

Risk capital

You have to understand that the stock market is a very volatile place and anything can happen within a matter of a few seconds. You have to be prepared for anything that it throws at you. In order to prepare for it, you have to make use of risk capital. Risk capital refers to money that you are willing to risk. You have to convince yourself that even if you lose the money that you have invested then it will not be a big deal for you. For that, you have to make use of your own money and not borrow from anyone, as you will start feeling guilty about investing it. Decide on a set number and invest it.

Research

You have to conduct a thorough research on the market before investing in it. Don't think you will learn as you go. That is only possible if you at least know the basics. You have to remain interested in gathering information that is crucial for your investments and it will only come about if you put in some hard work towards it. Nobody is asking you to stay up and go through thick text books. All you have to do is go through books and websites and gather enough information to help you get started on the right foot.

Diversification

You have to stress on diversification in your portfolio. You don't want all the money to go into the same place. Think of it as a way to increase your stock's potential. You have to choose different sectors and diverse stocks to invest in. you should also choose one of the different types of investments as they all contribute towards attaining a different result. Diversification is mostly seen, as a tool to cut down on risk and it is best that you not invest any more than 5% in any one of the securities.

Stop loss

You have to understand the importance of a stop loss mechanism. A stop loss technique is used to safeguard an investment. Now say for example you invest $100 and buy shares priced at $5 each. You have to place a stop loss at around $4 in order to stop it from going down any further. Now you will wonder as to why you have to place the stop loss and undergo one, well, by doing so, you will actually be saving your money to a large extent. You won't have to worry about the value slipping further down and can carry on with your trade.

Take a loss

It is fine to take a loss from time to time. Don't think of it as a big hurdle. You will have the chance the convert the loss into a profit. You have to remain confident and invested. You can take a loss on a bad investment that was anyway not going your way. You can also take a loss on an investment that you think is a long hold and will not work for you in the short term. Taking a few losses is the only way in which you can learn to trade well in the market.

These form the different dos of the stock market that will help you with your intraday trades.

Don'ts of day trading

No planning

Do not make the mistake of going about investing in the market without a plan in tow. You have to plan out the different things that you will do in the market and go about it the right way. This plan should include how much you will invest in the market, where you will invest, how you will go about it etc. No planning will translate to getting lost in the stock market, which is not a good sign for any investor.

Over rely on a broker

You must never over rely on a broker. You have to make your own decisions and know what to do and when. The broker will not know whether an investment is good for you. He will only be bothered about his profits. If he is suggesting something, then you should do your own research before investing in the stock. The same extends to emails that you might receive through certain sources. These emails are spams and meant to dupe you. So, don't make the mistake of trusting everything that you read.

Message boards

You have to not care about message boards. These will be available on the Internet and are mostly meant to help people gather information. But there will be pumpers and bashers present there. Pumpers will force people to buy a stock just to increase their value and bashers will force people to sell all their stocks just because they want the value to go down. Both these types are risky, as they will abandon the investors just as soon as their motive is fulfilled. So you have to be quite careful with it.

Calculate wrong

Some people make the mistake of calculating wrong. They will not be adept at math and will end up with wrong figures. This is a potential danger to all those looking to increase their wealth potential. If you are not good at calculating, then download n app that will do it for you or carry a calculator around to do the correct calculations. The motive is to make the right calculations and increase your wealth potential.

Copy strategies

Do not make the mistake of copying someone else's strategies. You have to come up with something that is your own and not borrowed from someone else. If you end up borrowing, then you will not be able to attain the desired results. You have to sit with your broker and come up with a custom strategy that you can employ and win big.

These form the different don'ts of the stock market that will help you keep troubles at bay.

CHAPTER 3
Day Trading Vs Swing Trading

A basic question to start with is this one - what are you looking for as a day trader? The answer here is quite easy.

First, you must look for stocks that are following a predictable trend. Then, you need to trade them in one single day. You don't need to keep them longer than a day. If you purchase stocks of Amazon (AMZN) today, you should not hold the stocks overnight and sell them tomorrow. It is no longer day trading if you hold on to your position. That one is called swing trading.

As a day trader, you need to understand the difference between day trading and swing trading. The latter is a type of trading in which you hold the stocks over a certain period of time, usually from one day to several weeks. This is a different style of trading, and you must not use these tools and strategies that are ideal for day trading if you want to follow the swing trading style.

Remember, day trading is a business (Rule 2). Swing trading is also a business, albeit a totally different type of business. The differences between day trading and swing trading are similar to the differences between owning a meat processing plant and a hamburger chain.

Both businesses involve food, but these are not similar. They operate with different revenue models, market segments, regulations, and time frames. You must not confuse day trading with other trading styles just because the trades are performed in the stock market.

Professional day traders close their positions before the stock market closes. Many traders perform both swing trading and day trading. They are aware that they are running two different businesses, and they are trained to manage the risks of these two types of trading.

One of the main differences between swing trading and day trading is the style of choosing stocks. Many traders do not day trade and swing trade the same stocks. Swing traders often look for stocks in established companies that they know will not lose their value in a few weeks.

But for day trading, you can trade any stock you want including companies that are predicted to go bankrupt. Day traders don't care what happens to the stocks after the market closes.

As a matter of fact, many of the companies that you day trade are quite risky to hold overnight because they may lose much of their value in a short period of time.

Before you begin to trade, you need to determine how active you want to be. You need to ask yourself questions like: how much time do I have at hand, and what are my current responsibilities? Your answers to these questions will help you to decide if you want to trade daily or if you want to buy and hold for some days or weeks.

There are two groups of active traders: the day traders and the swing traders. Both groups have a similar goal of making profits from short term or long term trades. However, there are major differences between the two that you should understand and make your decision on your best choice depending on your level of technical expertise, time frames, and your preference.

Basically, day trading is a form of trading where your long or short position is entered and exited on the same day- opens and closes within 24hours. Day traders get into positions based on quantitative, fundamental, or technical reasons. Day traders do not hold their positions overnight. Swing trading, on the other hand, is a long term investment where the trader buys or shorts securities and holds them for some days, weeks, or months. Unlike day traders, the swing traders do not intend to take trading as a full-time job.

Also, you do not need to have lots of capital to swing trade, while day trading follows the 'pattern day trader rule.' This rule is what governs any trader that makes more than four trades in the same security over five business days. This trader is referred to as "pattern day trader" based on the premise that the trades represent above 6% of the trader's total trading activity in that period. A pattern day trader must also have a minimum of $25,000 equity in their account on any trading day.

Day trading

Being a day trader can be very beneficial; however, it has its inherent risks. A day trader needs to realize that there may be times where he may encounter a 100% loss.

Day trading, more than some other type of trading, requires quick and right choices on positions and estimating the entry, exits, and stop-losses. The trades are fast and must be amazingly precise. Day trading imperatively requires being available and comprehending whatever occurs in the market at every point in time. Even though it doesn't imply that one should trade every day or consistently, the evaluations need to be done frequently. This type of trading takes more time than swing trading. However, it can be satisfying all-day work.

Day trading is better for people who have a passion for full-time trading and possess discipline, decisiveness, and diligence. For one to be successful as a day trader, he needs to have an in-depth understanding of charts and technical trading. Day trading can be stressful and intense, and so, traders need to be able to control their emotions and stay calm under fire.

Swing trading

A swing trader identifies swings in currencies, commodities, and stocks that occur over days. Unlike day trading, a swing trade may take up to weeks to work out. Swing traders have more persistence concerning their trade opening. As the positions extend to the second day, there is potential for huge benefits on a single trade, yet there are fewer trading opens generally. Anyone who has the investment capital and knowledge can give a shot at swing trading.

Swing trading requires less technical investigative abilities and progressively focus research and information on macroeconomics. The entry focus does not need to be that exact, and the planning isn't so pivotal since the moves which swing traders are expecting to get are bigger.

Swing trading doesn't require the trader to put in much time as frequent technical evaluation and consistent sitting before the screen is not necessary. It is usually a stress-free and low-effort job. The swing trader can have a separate full-time job as he does not have to stay glued to his computer screen all day.

Swing trades usually require time to work out. The more time a trade is open for days or week, the more the chances of having higher profits than trading multiple times daily on the same security. Margin requirements in a swing trade are higher since positions are held overnight. Compared to day trading whose maximum leverage is four times one's capital, swing trading is often two times the trader's capital.

Be that as it may, traders need to understand and utilize stop-losses and target levels to their benefit. While there is the possibility that the stop order will execute at an unfavorable price, it is still better than having to monitor all your open positions constantly.

As is normal with all types of trading, a swing trader can also experience losses, and because the traders hold the positions for a longer time, they may experience greater loss than the day traders.

Swing trading does not require the use of state of the art technology. You can swing trade with one computer, and any needed trading tools.

Because swing trading is usually not a full-time job, the traders have other sources of income and have reduced chances of burnout caused by stress.

When should you go for day trading?

The points below have summarized the ideal situation for you to be a day trader:

You are disciplined, diligent, and strong-willed.

You are willing to make small profits daily by making small trades.

You have the minimum capital requirements stated by FINRA rules for pattern day traders and SEC, if and when they apply to you.

You are knowledgeable and have the expertise to make great profits.

You are not easily stressed, and you can manage stress.

You are committed to studying current trends and can take needed action at the speed of light.

You never have a dull day, and you are out for excitement every minute.

When should you go for swing trading?

The points below have summarized the ideal situation for you to be a swing trader:

You lack extreme levels of technical understanding

You do not want to go full time into trading. That is, you don't desire trading as your only source of income.

You do not like stress and will instead go for something that is not as risky as day trading.

You do not fancy constant monitoring of market activities.

You are patient and can wait for weeks to months while studying the movements of the market.

You have a full-time job and can't spare time for day trading activities.

You do not have plenty of money to invest.

CHAPTER 4
The Main Tools used in Day Trading

Day Trading prediction techniques

There are certain Day trading techniques or tools (as we like to call them) that you can utilize to forecast the pattern that the stocks will follow.

1. Candlesticks

These are the most widely used techniques of prediction.

2. Fibonacci numbers

The mathematical technique that is utilized to predict stocks is the Fibonacci technique. Once you know how a Fibonacci series works, you will find it easy to comprehend. Your securities and stocks will follow a Fibonacci pattern and this will help you identify where it will stop next. Using this knowledge, you can choose either to stay or withdraw.

3. Rebate trading

Rebate trading is a popular technique. In this technique, you will be trading via an electronic communication network. These ECNs have been constructed to help people invest their money with ease. Once everybody's money is pooled together, the ECN will invest it in the stock market. It is found to be safe and helpful.

4. Range trading

Range trading is another good prediction technique. It is necessary to have boundaries and work within a range. To do this you will have to set limits to your investments. You can choose your limits.

5. Price action

In price action technique we make predictions by looking at the current prices. The trader makes some assumptions. If he thinks that those prices are falling and will continue to fall, he won't invest in them. If he feels those prices are rising and will continue to rise, he will not invest in it. This is an extremely safe approach and works only if one pays close attention to the trends.

6. Contrarian trading

Contrarian trading means doing the opposite of what the crowd is doing. Here, you buy stocks when people are selling them and sell stocks when people are buying them. This risk usually pays off but you need to know when to carry it out.

7. News forecasts

You should keep track of the news articles to be aware of the changes that are occurring in the company. If the share value is going up the company announces profits and dividends. On the other hand, if the share value will go down the company announces that it has undergone a loss and the steps it will take to minimize the effect of the loss or how they will rebuild. You need to work with this knowledge.

Software

There are different kinds of software that will help you with your stock investments. You have to see which works best for you. They help you read and predict the trends. This software can be installed by you on your own or with the help of a friend or broker.

The other essentials tools are a good computer or laptop, good telephone connection and a fast Internet connection.

Importance of using these day trading tools:

These are the different prediction techniques that you must take into account to be successful in day trading. You can choose any of these day trading tools to help you in your venture. In today's world, you cannot expect to succeed without the help of these tools. You require technology to assist you in your trades.

Some of the benefits of these tools are:

- Gives you an edge over other investors in the market.
- Will help you save time and energy
- Will help in the formation an advantageous strategy and increase your chances of being successful.

How Fibonacci numbers can help you trade better:

8. Some academics agree that Fibonacci numbers are powerful in financial markets.
9. These numbers offer a framework for evaluating price action
10. These numbers are watched by traders and provide key horizontal price levels.
11. These price levels tend to bring higher levels or more volume and thus, can lead to a promising trade setup.

Ever come across this saying that a day trader is only as fine as the tools they are working with? In this chapter, we shall take a look at the different tools used in day trading.

Best Software for Day Trading.

A day trading software is a term given to any software that can help in the decision making and analysis in order to make a trade. Some of the software will provide you with accessibility to the tools and all the resources needed.

A day trading software has the following basic features:

- Any software should have the functionality of allowing the set-up of trading strategy in the system.
- Possess the order-placing function which is normally automated.
- Tools for continuous assessment of the market developments so as to act on them.

How does trading software works?

Day trading software can be divided into four different categories:

- Charting. Bright day traders will normally chart their prices using different charting software. However, some outside vendors normally offer feeds with charting packages which help in the analysis of technical indicators. Most of these data feeds are normally advanced packages.
- Data. Before any day trader begins trading, you should be aware of the prices of the stocks, its future, and current currencies.
- Execution of trade. After sourcing for the data and analyzed it on a chart, at some point, a day trader will need to enter into trade. Trade execution requires some sort of trading software. A good number of trading software nowadays allow you to develop your own trading strategies using APIs (Application Programming Interface). Some even specifically provide trading capabilities that are automated for day training.

Below are some of the platforms for day trading you can select.

- Zacks Trade.

Zacks Trade is a brokerage day trading platform mostly for the US and international consumers. It started its trading since 2014 and its offices are suited in Chicago.

This online platform is mostly for active traders and investors. Investors on this trading platform need to make a deposit of around $2500 for them to register an account with the broker. However, if you are seeking help to make a trade, Zacks is the best choice for you since it offers brokerage trades for free. The tradable securities involved on this platform include market stocks, exchange-traded funds, and bonds. On this platform, you can make market trades more than 91 exchanges in different countries.

The cost per share of the commission is around $0.01 with a minimum of $3. This platform is mostly preferred to the active and options traders, investors seeking to trade on foreign stock exchanges and also those who want to access a human broker.

Zacks Trade offers two types of accounts; Zacks Trade Pro normally for the active users and Zacks Trader for the retail traders. Zacks Trader has a simple user interface, therefore, making it easy for the users to navigate through the system. The pros of this software are that:

- It is quite rare to find a trading platform that offers cheap commission such as a cent. To engage in trading the penny stocks, you will need to pay around 1% of the trade's value with a minimum cost of $3. The cost for options is around $3 for the first contract and cost of additional ones which is 75 cents.
- Zacks normally offers investors with the accessibility to 26 research and 87 reports on subscriptions.

- ▢   This software is also available for Linux users. Account-holders can also access Zacks using their mobile phones unlike it is seen on other software.
- ▢   Zacks Trade is so safe and secure. Clients normally have their own platforms from the management and they register for their accounts with unique usernames and passwords.
- ▢   Good customer service. This platform enables day traders who use their smartphones to trade for a free 24/7 hour basis. It is mostly for traders suited in Asia, the US, and Australia.

The shortcoming for this software is that it offers slightly higher charges on shares as compared to Interactive brokers.

- •   Interactive Brokers.

This software is strongly advisable for advanced and frequent traders. It charges $0.01 per share with no minimum investment required. It offers a wide range of investments such as European bonds for the government and the corporate. Interactive brokers offer research for free to its traders from around 100 providers such as Zacks and many more.

The advantages of this software include:

- ▢   The low commission charges on exchange-traded funds and stock tend to favor the frequent traders. The low rates also favor the margin traders.
- ▢   Interactive Broker's workstation is fast and offers great features such as watchlists, real-time monitoring, and advanced charting.
- ▢   Another great advantage of Interactive Broker is that it offers its traders massive accessibility to research and news services which keeps them up to date.

The greatest shortcoming of Interactive Brokers is that traders find it hard to navigate through the website. This makes it difficult for traders to identify the costs associated with the commissions and fees.

- •   TD Ameritrade.

This is one of the largest trading brokerage software with the basic and Thinkorswim platforms. It charges fees of $6.95 per share and no minimum investment is required. The Thinkorswim platform allows clients to customize color schemes and layouts according to their choice of preference. Trade tickets are found on both of the platforms so a trader can enter an order in whichever platform you are using.

After the software development team made updates on the tools and content of this software, there has been an improved look on both of the platforms making it more responsive to the client's devices.

TD Ameritrade offers a range of tradable securities; over 300 exchange-traded funds are free of charge and over 12,000 mutual funds. It also provides investors and traders accessibility to research for good quality trade execution especially for traders using the Thinkorswim platform.

The pros of TD Ameritrade include the following:

- ☐ Offers wide news and research abilities to the traders which keep them up to date.
- ☐ Provide a full range of investments such as forex and bitcoin futures trading for the right clients.
- ☐ Provide massive education support for the traders. There are videos and also articles that provide simple guidelines to the traders on how to use the tools provided. It is so difficult to find a trader who cannot use this software despite you being a guru or a newbie.
- ☐ TD Ameritrade offers mock trading accounts. Traders are given virtual money of around $100,000 for practice. Traders can back test trading strategies and access foreign futures.

The biggest shortcoming of TD Ameritrade is the high charges on commission and the exchange-traded funds as compared to other software.

- • TradeStation.

TradeStation is a day training software that charges $5 per share and requires a minimum investment of $500. It normally focuses on good quality data of the market and the trade executions. Its system is well established and normally remains firm during market surges. You can establish your own system using the analysis tools and mock testing strategies provided by this software.

The advantages of this software are as follows:

- ☐ The platform has minimal chances of crashing down since it is a stable platform.
- ☐ The software feature out excellent charting tools and back testing strategies making it the popular software.
- ☐ Education support for this software is at top-notch. It normally offers classes and educational videos to its traders on various topics such as margins and many others.

The shortcoming of this software is that there no cases of forex trading and international trading is limited.

- • eOption

eOption is another day trading software that focuses on quality. It has a minimum investment of $500 and charges $3 per trade. The massive number of fans of eOption is mostly after the low commission and the extreme faster trade executions.

You can check out the platform before opening the account by using Paper Trading Toolset which is given for free for around 45 days.

This software has various pros:

- ☐ It is easy for traders to navigate through the web-based platform. The user interface is so simple and the tools provided are easier to be found by the traders.

- ⬜ Good customer service. The platform is so stable and seldom has cases of crashing down.
- ⬜ The cost of using this software is very low since the charge per trade is $3. However, users for inactive accounts are normally charged an annual fee of $50.

The cons of this software are:
- ⬜ Limited accessibility for the traders to research and news providers unlike in other software.
- ⬜ Education support is not that good. The offerings are limited making it difficult for new traders.
  - Firstrade.

This is a trading software which is free of charge and requires a minimum investment of $0. It began offering $0 commission to traders dealing with options and the stock recently and for its benefit, it offered limited tools and research for the traders using this software. Firstrade also has this lending program which provides lending services to financial bodies and account holders and they can generate income. The traders can even sell the stock with no restrictions.

Some of the pros of this software include the following:
- ⬜ It provides a set of accounts. It has simplified English, traditional and even Chinese accounts.
- ⬜ It has lower costs. Charges $0 for the stock and options traders.
- ⬜ This software provides access to stocks, options and funds type of trading.

The drawbacks of this software include the following:
- ⬜ Firstrade does not provide access to forex, future and crypto type of trading.
- ⬜ It does not have a 24/7 basis for customer support. They only operate in limited hours as compared to other brokerage trading platforms.
- ⬜ This platform has a few functionalities for its traders. Its traders are forced to use functionality from other platforms.
  - TradingView.

This is a trading software that is free, also has monthly charges of $9.95 for the Pro account, $19.95 for the Pro+ account and $39.95 for the premium account. Trading View does not support stock options and U.S trading.

A trader can make trades on the charts and the software will work out for you the profit and loss reports and analysis.

Its advantages include the following:
- ⬜ This software is of ease of use even to beginners.
- ⬜ Offer support for a variety of trades such as stock, forex, and cryptocurrency.

- The charting for this software is easy to use and provides you with various tools.

The disadvantage of this software that turns many off is that it has no real-time news for the traders, unlike other trading software.

Tools and Services Used for Day Trading

For an effective job in day trading, a trader is required to possess a set of tools and services. Some of the tools required are the basic ones that you already possess such as a laptop or computer and a telephone.

Other tools that a trader may need include a charting platform and also real-time data. The tools and services needed by a day trader to be on the move include the following:

- Laptop or computer.

Technology nowadays keeps on changing rapidly. A trader should at least possess a good laptop or computer with excellent memory and processors. A good computer processor will speed up the trade executions for excellent trade results. Also, a machine with high memory will have the capability of backing up the market data and there will be minimal chances of the computer crashing down.

- Charting software.

Day trading software provided by companies or outside vendors normally have different features. Some software has charting platforms where traders can keep track of the price changes of the stock. Price charts make work easier for traders making their work effective and efficient. Software that lacks charting platforms makes it tough for new traders making contributing to slow trades. A day trader should mostly prefer software with charting platforms.

- Internet.

Internet is one of the crucial resources required by online users. The Internet with fast speed produces effective work. A trader is able to be up-to-date with the current prices in the market. Workflow also becomes smooth since there is no lagging behind web pages unlike it is seen on slow internet. A trader should, of course, set high priorities for service providers with good internet speeds for excellent works.

- Telephone.

In case you need to cut down the costs of the internet, a trader is advised to possess a cell phone or a landline. A telephone will assist you in contacting your broker in case your offline. You will need to back up the broker's contact number on your telephone for assistance.

- Real-time market data.

Market data constitute of prices and markets you choose to trade. The market can be futures, options, forex, and even stocks. It is upon you as a trader to decide on the type of market you want and contacts your broker. Some brokers offer all the market data for free but with high commission.

☐ Broker.

A day trading broker can be a company or small brokers. A broker provides a trader with the necessary market trades according to your choice of preference. Different brokers provide software with different features. Some may include platforms with all trades others with limited trades. Software with all trades most times requires payment of high commission ending up being a big burden for the inactive and small traders. It is mostly advisable to select smaller but regulated brokers who provide lower commissions.

Key Parameters in Day Trading

Despite the trading strategies, the key parameters in day trading to put into considerations are as follows:

☐ Day trading volume.

This is a great day trading metric that helps traders identify the liquidity of an asset. High day trading volume help traders enter and go out of position so faster and easier.

☐ Liquidity.

Liquidity is a crucial parameter for day traders who make profits from many trades. Traders normally monitor the trading volume of the market trade to determine its liquidity.

☐ Price volatility.

This is essential for traders to monitor the price fluctuations in the market. Traders are able to monitor profits from prices that are short term.

Essential Tools Used for Day Trading

The a-must tools that a serious day trader need to have included the following:

☐ Trading platform.

With the emergence of modern technology, online traders should possess online trading platforms. These platforms are normally provided by different companies and have different features. These platforms should be advanced and firm with no bugs. There is trading software available on smartphones and users can access anytime and anywhere. You should choose software that is cheaper and will not burden you.

☐ Monitors.

Having access to multiple computer monitors is an added advantage to a day trader. Computer monitors help in keeping track of the performances of the stock, price fluctuations, news and also the key parameters. This promotes the effective performance of a day trader in the market.

☐ News and data feed.

Possession of multiple computer monitors and an advanced trading platform will definitely keep the news and data feeds up to date. Out of date news feeds bring confusion and wrong information about the stock performance and prices in the market.

▢ Research skills.

A trader needs to have marvelous research skills. The skills will help you understand the capital for the stocks market and the key parameters needed for day trading.

▢ Faster Internet.

High-speed internet is so crucial for any trader making a living with day trading. Such a kind of Internet makes work easier since trade executions become faster. Day traders normally require up-to-date news and data feeds and therefore slow-speed internet is so risky for online day traders.

▢ Capital.

Like any other kind of business, capital is a required necessity. Day traders need sufficient capital for the trading volume. This will enable traders to manage their volumes accordingly for better profits.

CHAPTER 5
Choosing the Right Stocks to Trade

There are thousands of equities available for a trader to choose from, and day traders have no limit on the type of stocks they can trade; you can trade on virtually any stock of your choice. With all these available choices, it may seem like a difficult task to know the right stock to add to your watchlist. This takes us to the first step in day trading, which is knowing what to trade.

Here are some tips that will help you to choose the best stocks for maximum profits:

1. High Volatility and Liquidity in Day Trading

Liquidity in financial markets refers to how one can quickly buy or sell an asset in the market. It can also mean the impact that trading has on the price of a security. It is easier to day trade liquid stocks than other stocks; they are also more discounted, which makes them cheaper.

Liquid stocks are bigger in volume, in the sense that one can purchase and sell larger quantities of stock without having any significant effect on the price. Because day trading strategies depend on accurate timing and speed, a lot of volume makes it easier for traders to get in and out of trades. Depth is also important as it shows you the level of liquidity of stocks at different price levels below or above the current market offer and bid.

Also, corporations with higher market capitalizations have more liquid equities than those with lower market caps because it is easier to find sellers and buyers for stocks owned by these big corporations.

Stocks that have more volatility also follow the day trading strategies. A stock is considered volatile if the corporation that owns it experiences more adjustment in its cash flow. Uncertainty in the financial market creates a big opportunity for day trading. Online financial services like Google Finance or Yahoo Finance regularly list highly volatile and liquid stocks during the day. This information is also available on other online broker sites.

2. Consider Your Own Position

The stocks you decide to go for have to align with your goals and personal situation because there is no one-size-fits-all in the financial market. You have to put into consideration your capital, your risk appetite, and the type of investing you are going to take on. Let's not forget the role of research in all these. Your best bet is to read up on financials of different companies, study the market, consider the sectors that best reflect your values, personality, and personal needs, and remember to begin early. You need to be familiar with the market openings and time yourself to follow these openings. While day trading, ensure not to get emotionally attached to a particular stock. Don't forget that you are looking at patterns to know when best to exit or enter to minimize your losses and increase your profit. While you do not have to stay glued to your screen, you still need to know the earning season and what the economic calendar looks like. This will help you to pick the best stocks for day trading.

3. Social Media

This industry is also another attractive target for day trading as there are several online media companies like Facebook and LinkedIn, that have high trading volume for their stocks.

Also, there have been several debates on the capability of these social media companies to convert their massive user bases into a sustainable income stream. Although stock prices, in theory, represent the discounted cash flow of the companies that issued them, the recent valuations also look at the earning potential of these companies. Based on this, some analysts think that this has led to higher stock valuation than is suggested by the fundamentals. Regardless, social media is still a popular stock for day trading.

4. Financial Services

Financial services industries also offer great stocks for day trading. For example, Bank of America is one of the most highly traded stocks per trading session. If you are looking for company stock to day trade, stocks from Bank of America should be among your top consideration, despite the increased skepticism that the banking system is facing. The trading volume for Bank of America is high, which makes it a liquid stock. This also applies to Morgan Stanley, Citigroup, JP Morgan & Chase, and Well Fargo. They all have uncertain industrial conditions and high trading volumes.

5. Going Outside Your Geographical Boundary

When trading in the financial market, you must diversify your portfolio. Look at stocks listed in other exchanges like the London Stock Exchange (LSE) or Hong Kong's Hang Seng. Extending your portfolio outside your boundary will grant you access to potentially cheaper alternatives as well as foreign stocks.

6. Medium to high instability

A day trader needs to understand the price movement to be able to make money. As a day trader, you can choose to go for stocks that typically move a lot in percentage terms or dollar terms, as these two terms usually yield different results. Stocks that typically move 3% and above every day have a consistently large intraday moves to trade. This also applies to stocks that move above $1.50 each day.

7. Group followers

Although some traders specialize in contrarian plays, most traders will rather go for equities that move in line with their index and sector group. What this means is that, when the sector or index ticks upward, the price of individual stocks will also increase. This is crucial if the trader desires to trade the weakest or strongest stocks every day. If a trader will rather go for the same stock every day, then it is advisable to focus on that stock and worry less on whether it corresponds with any other thing.

Entry and Exit Strategies

After you must have picked the best stocks in the world, your strategies will determine if you will profit from them or not. There are several available day trading strategies, but to increase your chances of success, you need to stick to certain guidelines and look out for certain intraday trading signals.

Below, I will talk about 5 of these guidelines:

1. Trade Weak Stocks in a Downtrend and Strong Stocks in an Uptrend

Most traders, in a bid to pick the best stocks for day trading, prefer to look at EFTs or equities that have at least a moderate to high connection with the Nasdaq or S&P 500 indexes, and then separate the strong stocks from the weak ones. This creates an opportunity for the day trader to make profit as the strong stock has the potential to go 2% up when the index moves 1% up. The more a stock moves, the more opportunity for the day trader.

As market futures/ indexes move higher, traders should purchase stocks that have more aggressive upward movement than the futures. With this, even if the futures pull back, it will have little or no impact/ pull back on a strong stock. These are the stocks you should trade in an uptrend as they provide more profit potential when the market goes higher.

When the futures or indexes drop, it becomes profitable to short sell those stocks that drop more than the market. The ETFs and stocks that are weaker or stronger than the market may change each day, however, certain sectors may be relatively weak or strong for weeks at a time. When looking for a stock to trade, always go for the strongr one. This same rule applies to short trades as well. As a short seller, you should isolate EFTs or stocks that are weaker so that when prices fall, you will have greater chances of having profits by being in EFTs or stocks that fall the most.

2. Trade Only with the current intraday Trend

The trading market always moves in waves, and its your job as a trader to ride these waves. When there is an uptrend, your focus should be on taking long positions while you should focus on taking short positions whenever there is a downtrend. We have already established that intraday trends do not go on forever but, you can carry out one or more trades before a reversal occurs. When there is a shift with the dominant trend, you should begin to trade with the new trend. It may be difficult to isolate the trend, but you can find simple and useful entry and stop loss strategies from Trendlines.

3. Take your time. Wait for the Pullback

Trendlines provide visual guides that show where price waves will start and end. So, when choosing stocks to day trade, you can use a trendline for early entry into the next price wave. When you want to enter a long position, be patient and wait for the price to move down towards the trendline and then move back higher before you buy. Before an upward trendline can appear, a price low before a higher price low needs to happen. A line is drawn to connect the two points and then extends to the right. This same principle applies when short selling. Be patient for the price to move up to the downward-slope trendline, and once the stock starts to move back down, you can then make your entry.

4. Take your profits regularly

As a day trader, you have limited time to make profits, and for this reason, you need to spend very little time in trades that are moving in the wrong direction or losing money. Let me show you two simple guidelines that you can use to take profits when trading with trends:

- In a short position or downtrend, take your profits slightly below or at the former price low in the current trend.
- In a long position or uptrend, take your profits at slightly above or at the former price high in the current trend.

5. Do not play when the market stalls

The market may not always trend. The intraday trends may reverse so often that it becomes hard to establish an overriding direction. If there are no major lows and highs, ensure the intraday movements are large enough to increase the chances of profits and reduce the risks of lose. For instance, if you are risking $0.15 per share, the EFT or stock should move enough to give you a minimum of $0.20 - $0.25 profit using the guidelines stated above. When the price is not trending (that is, moving in a range), move to a range-bound trading technique. During a range, you will no longer have an angled line, but rather a horizontal line. However, the general concept still applies: purchase only when the price goes to the lower horizontal area (support) and then begins to move higher. Short sell once you notice that the price has reached the upper horizontal line (resistance) and begins to go lower again.

Your buying strategy should be to exit close to the top of the range but not exactly at the top. Your shorting strategy should be to exit in the lower part of the range but not exactly at the bottom. The chances of making gains should be more than the risk of loss. Place a stop loss just above the most current high before entry on a short signal or just below the most current low before entry on a buy signal.

Several traders find it hard to alternate between range trading and trend trading and so they opt to do one or the other. If you choose to go for range trading, then you should avoid trading during trends, but focus on trading EFTs or stocks that tend to range. If trend trading on the other hand, avoid trading when the markets are ranging, and you should concentrate on trading EFTs or stocks that have the potential to trend.

CHAPTER 6
Psychology and Mindset

Day Trading, like any other form of investment, is subject to influence from human emotion and psychological impact. Whenever money or capital is in play, people tend to take matters rather personally because of the inevitable consequence of the hope that comes along with the promise of significant returns. People will strive to make money while at the same time, avoid circumstances that may cause them to lose their capital. It is from this zero-sum mentality that the influence of psychology or emotions may creep into a sensible mindset. Such control takes over every aspect of the Day Trading instincts that you learned over time.

Your knowledge goes out of the window when a situation that triggers your psychological response arises. A high degree of counterproductivity thus ensues. It, eventually, leads to the dismissal of logical decisions in favor of hunches as well as the need to chase after fleeting profits and cover your previous losses. For you to manage your Day Trading expertise through challenging scenarios, you need to look out for emotions that alter your reasoning capability adversely. Try to improve and nurture a productive mindset, while at the same time, avoid promoting a mental culture that justifies negativity falsely. The following few behaviors and traits are central to your particular mindset whenever you decide to participate in Day Trading:

Do Not Rationalize Your Trading Errors

This mindset t is one of the leading obstacles to the progress and eventual success of your Day Trading endeavors. You are often prone to justify any trading mistakes that you make to the detriment of moving forward. For instance, you get an entry into a particularly promising trade deal later than necessary in spite of your much earlier knowledge of its potential for profitability. The delay causes you to miss an excellent opportunity at the previous entry point. However, you decide to justify this misstep by convincing yourself of your preference for trading late over missing the same deal entirely.

The downside to such delays is often a faulty sense of size estimation in taking your trading position. Hence, the resulting increased exposure to financial risk you become disadvantaged by. Beware of your procrastination when it comes to productive openings that are currently available in Day Trading. If you possess this tendency, consider getting rid of it as soon as possible before it costs you a lot more capital in the long run. In case you are not prone to the frequent postponement of your responsibilities to a later date, be alert for the development of this mentality with the trading company that you keep. You can quickly become influenced by the kind of traders from whom you seek advice on more complex trading strategies. When present, stockbrokers affect your trading ethos, as well.

Poor trading etiquette from these external sources will rub off on you and vice versa. Try to keep the company of well-known responsible trading partners and stockbrokers when the need arises. Another rationalization scenario involves a run of profitable results. Based on a series of trade deals that made you successive returns, you begin to convince your brain of your seemingly high intelligence. This false belief in your skills may lead you to overestimate your trading expertise. Before long, you may start engaging in Day Trading on a hunch rather than apply logic to your decisions. You stop referring to your trusted trading plan and jump into many trading opportunities haphazardly. After a while, these instances of carelessness and trading arrogance will catch up with you because they always inevitably do. Your chances of plunging into a financial disaster go up.

With your eventual financial ruin come the cases of psychological meltdown leading to a negative feedback loop. A wrong decision from your misplaced sense of conceitedness will invariably lead to high-risk exposure. As a result, you suffer significant losses eventually, and consequently, your emotional health suffers, causing you to spiral into a state of depression. This loop is often self-propagating, meaning that it feeds onto itself. Bad decisions lead to adverse outcomes and a fragile mindset, which, in turn, is prone to make more bad decisions, and the loop goes on and on. Keep in mind that in Day Trading, such a feedback loop is often disastrous. All these adverse effects arise from your initial false sense of justification for a wrong deed.

Beware of Your Trading Decisions

This advice is so apparent that it sounds redundant when mentioned. However, decisions are typically the product of your reasoning and judgment at a particular moment. When it comes to decisions on Day Trading, psychological influence is often a determining factor in the process. Keeping your wits about you is very crucial, especially when everything seems to be out of control. You need to realize that every trade has its ups and downs and how you deal with the challenging times is often more consequential. Try to maintain a logical mindset when making Day Trading choices from a variety of bad options. When it seems that an imminent financial downturn is inevitable, the extent of your loss becomes essential. In this case, you will need to make a sensible decision on the degree of losing margins that you can tolerate adequately.

At this point, you are probably in a state of so many overwhelming emotions that your foggy mental faculties become clouded. An expected human response is to run away from danger, naturally, but in certain situations, fleeing may not be an option. A reflex in a trading scenario often leads to an impulsive decision. Such a choice is, in turn, typically not well thought or deliberative. You should confront your unfavorable circumstances head-on and attempt to fix the situation, however hopeless. This sense of perseverance is usually the essence of most trading excursions, especially when the times become financially rough. Going through the loss of some capital and other Day Trading challenges is often a painful experience that can lead to illogical decisions.

Always remember to uphold vigilance and adhere strictly to the guidelines in your trading plan when confronted with obstacles during your trades. The trading plan usually has instructions on how to handle these seemingly desperate situations. In addition, the prior preparation of any trading guide is generally free of emotional or psychological influence; hence, you can rely on it to maintain neutrality. Also, beware of making trading resolutions when going through a phase with a foul mood. Such conclusions are bound to lead you into a financial catastrophe, especially if you are not careful. Learn to put off the verdict to a time when you can resume logical thinking. When you make any rash decision, it can only result in your further exposure to even more risk.

Keep Your Emotions in Check

Learn to stick to a Day Trading system and method that you trust. Such a strategy may be one that has a history of always making significant returns. Once you master and fully grasp how to apply a specific approach to your trading deals, try to fine-tune it to your preference based on your ultimate objectives. Afterward, stick to this tried, practiced, and tested system in all your searches for valid trade deals. On some days, the stock market may be slow with a low volume of trade. The volatility in such a case is often negligible. However, due to an unchecked emotional influence, you develop a sense of greed or lust for profits.

The desire for benefits on a slow day is common. It leads to the urge to trade on anything to make a small profit. In this situation, you will move from Day Trading into gambling. Trading requires a logical mindset on your part with a lack of psychological attachment whatsoever. Gambling is a consequence of emotional and mental factors running amok in your Day Trading system. If a particular trading style worked on multiple times in the past, teach your brain to consider it. Your trusted trading system will indicate a lack of valid trade opportunities on a specific slow market day. In this case, curb your emotions, desires, and urges to chase a quick profit; however strong they seem.

You should never allow yourself to resort to gambling under any circumstances. Gambling is detrimental to healthy and responsible Day Trading behavior. The risk exposure exponentially rises when you grow accustomed to the desire for profits. If a given day of trading is unfavorable, you should not take part in invalid and unworthy deals. In addition, you should only trade on verifiable opportunities. At certain times, you may experience a series of successive returns in a relatively short period. Learn to know when to stop and how to curb your lust for wanting more returns. Trust your system to trade only on valid deals;

however, multiple opportunities are available. An emotion that goes unmonitored in such situations is the greed for more profit.

You convince yourself psychologically that the various deals could be a sign of your lucky day. This mentality in a false belief is wrong, and you need to be aware of it. Your psychology can play deceitful tricks on your logical mind leading to high-risk trading deals. You must realize that in Day Trading, it is almost impossible to get more returns out of a system than what the stock market offers. Emotional corruption also comes into play in a scenario where you bite off more than you can chew.

The greed for substantial amounts of returns may cause you to take high-risk trading positions for a chance at quick profits. However, you must remember that profits and losses are both possible outcomes from a Day Trading session. Therefore, you need to learn to trade in amounts that you can afford to lose. After all, Day Trading involves taking a chance based on a speculative position. You should practice trading in small amounts of money within the confines of low-risk deals. In this case, a potential loss may not be as damaging as the earlier high-risk trading position driven by greed. Eliminate the role of emotions in Day Trading and learn to accept the uncertainty of an unknown future outcome.

Be Patient When Trading

Patience is a crucial trait to have when you take part in Day Trading due to the upswings and downward trends in stock prices. It can become challenging to identify the right entry or exit point for a particular trading opportunity, given the fluctuating nature of a volatile market. However, when you master the art of being patient and studying the trade intently, you can come up with a winning strategy. Having a planned approach is essential, and you should prepare one before engaging in any Day Trading. Often, most seasoned traders include trading strategies for different market conditions in their trading plans. Hence, when making your trading plan, consider incorporating a trading strategy within it.

If unsure of how to proceed, you can always seek the assistance of qualified stockbrokers. They have the experience of encountering various Day Trading scenarios in the real world. If trustworthy, they could provide you with invaluable insights on coming up with a proper strategy. Now it is up to you to stick to the plan in every session in which you participate. Patience demands that you pay attention to the planned strategy and ignore any attractive distractions when trading. For instance, a brief upswing from a potential price action breakout may be misleading. It might cause you to falsely believe that the stock price is about to pick momentum and keep rising on the chart.

However, as attractive as this scenario might be, a sense of diligent patience demands that you ignore it and refer to your strategy. Upon referral to your trading plan strategy, you may encounter the concept of false breakouts. You also learn that these false upswings in trend usually follow a prolonged period of price consolidated. As a result, your patience allows you to evade a potentially wrong entry point to a trading position. You are also able to pick the right exit point from a particular trading session based on strategic patience. The price action chart acts merely as a guide for your trading actions and not the determining factor.

How do you combat a troubled trading mindset?

You would have to make a trading plan and stick to it. This plan aims to have an honest assessment and understanding of the trader's action. You also need to define your trading methodology. You would have to master your emotions in order to seize the profits.

Self- confidence is an important attributes. If you lack confidence then it would show in your deals. Without confidence, you are not likely to trust and follow something that have developed. Successful trading relies on decision making. Because of money and natural instincts, people cannot remove their emotions from their decision making process. You also need to be discipline with your decision making and focusing on the right areas. There are traders who tend to shed much of their energy thinking about the wrong things.

What the market does to you is not important. The market may lose or may profit today, but what is important is how you react to the market. Trading psychology may be made by some losing traders as their excuse, but bottom line is, a healthy trading mindset gives profitable results.

What is Trading Psychology?

Trading psychology is the change in mindset, emotion and perception, and thus behavior, when pursuing active, "live" trades, as opposed to demos. Trading one's own money, or managing other people's investments adds a psychological element and added barrier to success that cannot be duplicated in the classroom. Emotions, such as indecision, fear and greed, which normally do not come into play during the training process, crop up when one begins to trade with actual money. These emotions result from not only the use of real money, but the highly stressful and competitive environment of the day trading floor. Learning how to identify and manage these psychological elements will allow you to retain a clearer head and make better trading decisions.

Why is it Important?

When in training, taking the risk of putting one's money on a company or fund is pretty easy. It is a bit like playing Monopoly, you make decisions with fake money that are much harder to make when real money is at stake. Easy decisions in training can easily start to feel like rocket science to the new trader. Indecision or rash decision making can result from being flustered as a result of the stress and reality of the trading floor. These poor decisions can lead one to losing out on a good trading opportunity or going "all in" before you have had enough time to really think it through.

Besides indecision, fear and greed are the biggest psychological barriers to good trading. These emotions can quickly and negatively impact your ability to make quality, well thought trading decisions. Fear can cause an inability to make a move or maintain patience until a trade gets to its most profitable level. Greed can cause one to make risky trading decisions to get that "big hit" and cause you to lose a lot of money, fast.

What Can I Do to Maintain Positive Trading Psychology?

It is important to reduce your stress levels and manage your emotions while trading. This can be really difficult in the heat of the pressure of rapidly changing trading situations that you must quickly react to. One of the best things you can do to maintain your cool is to create a trading plan that has different contingencies for various possible market changes and stick to your plan. By creating a plan of action while in a cool mindset, you can avoid the negative ramifications of making a rash decision that you do not have time to properly think through. Focus on educating yourself and keeping up to date with the most effective trading strategies. You need to develop the ability to be more flexible in your planning, while keeping an eye towards responsible risk management. Having this solid plan that accounts for various different possibilities gives you the ability to make on the floor decisions without allowing your emotions to control your choices.

While it might not seem like psychological concepts would come into play when talking about trading, psychology is us, and it is everywhere. Having an understanding of the psychology of trading, and how best to manage your emotions and psychological pitfalls that can negatively impact your ability to make good trades, will improve the quality of your trading decisions. Learning how to manage the psychology of trading is part and parcel to the successful trader as you can be your own biggest asset, as well as your own worst enemy.

Where True Trading Confidence Comes From

Developing enduring confidence in your real-time trading skills and abilities doesn't come overnight. It's a process. And, it's the process of 'getting there' that we focus on to improve and to "be a good trader." Confidence comes from mastering the various skills needed to read the market, execute and manage trades. Mastering these skills and abilities is the process of trading and it is this process that brings about confidence. Confidence really doesn't come from more winning trades. In fact, more winning trades come from a dedicated focus on the process.

How to Maintain Improvement and Add to Confidence

A key to both building self-confidence and maintaining skills and abilities that you have already developed thus far is to understand how we learn. Although we can certainly learn quickly, learning can't be rushed. This is especially true with the multifaceted skill sets needed in trading. Far too often I see traders try a strategy or indicator, have a loss or two, and drop that strategy like a hot potato. Again, their focus is on results. This flawed mindset will only frustrate you; lasting improvement and true confidence will always be elusive.

Learning is not linear. It does not happen in a straight line. We don't start at point A and steadily advance to point B. Instead, learning occurs in a series of ups, downs, and plateaus. It is very much like the swings that occur in an up trend. We experience spurts of growth and development, fall back a bit, advance some more, and then rest a while as we hit a new plateau where what we consolidate what have learned.

Traders with the misguided mindset are thrilled with the ups, get depressed with the downs, and become bored with plateaus. Again, their focus is on results. How can anyone develop genuine confidence on such a roller coaster?

Where Trading Confidence is Really Found

Confidence is found in the learning plateaus where our gains are consolidated and our abilities stabilize. Confidence isn't found in the ups because that is not our true skill level. The learning hasn't had time to take hold. The downs of our learning curve aren't places to become scared or depressed. The downs are to be welcomed. Why? Because this is where we learn what additionally we need to become better. Where else would we get this crucial information? And the plateaus aren't the place to become bored; they are to be savored.

Trading confidence comes from dedicated focus on the process of trading. One of the best ways to focus on the process is by reviewing your trading each day and each week.

Forex Trading Psychology - Getting the Mindset of the Millionaire Traders

Forex trading can be learned by anyone yet 95% of traders lose and most don't fail because they can't learn but because they simply cannot get the right mindset. Forex trading requires a different mindset to succeed and we will discuss how to get a winning mindset in this article...

In a famous trading experiment trading legend Richard Dennis taught a group of people with no trading experience, to trade in just 14 days. The result was they went onto make hundreds of millions in profits and go down in trading history.

The key to the experiment was not the method this was a simple long term breakout method but giving the people the mindset to apply it with discipline. In interviews with the traders they all pointed to the fact learning the method was easy, but applying the method through periods of losses, was the hard part.

Trading discipline is often seen as the key to success and it is. The reason you need it is you must ride out inevitable periods of losses and keep executing your trading signals, until you hit profits again.

You don't just get discipline, it's based upon certain other traits which are as follows.

1. Acceptance of Responsibility

Your financial future is in your hands, no one else can make you money, you are responsible for your success or failure.

2. Forex Education

You need to work smart and learn the right information and avoid the numerous myths that causes losses. From this education, you can develop a simple Forex trading strategy for success and as you have done your homework you will have the next trait.

3. Confidence

You will only be disciplined if you know what you are doing and are confident in what you are doing - there are still some other hurdles to overcome to get discipline and they are keeping your emotions out of trading and for this, you need to do the following:

4. Keeping Your Emotions at Bay

Do not give or seek advice. Stay away from the crowd and follow your own path; the crowd always losses and being on your own maybe lonely in real life but in Forex it's the way to win.

Leave your ego behind and accept you will lose at times. This is not a failing on your part, its just part of trading reality. Get frustrated or angry at the market and you will veer off course, so be humble take your losses cheerfully and know your day will come.

Keep this in Mind: Traders are always trying to use technology to beat the market and all the time, we see new complex theories that are supposed to beat simple ones - but they don't help. Despite all the advances we have seen over the last 50 years, the ratio of winners to losers remains the same and the route to success is the same as it's always been:

A simple, logical, robust trading system, which you understand, have confidence in and can apply with a disciplined mindset.

Learning to trade Forex is easy, getting the right mindset is the hard part - but you can get the mindset of a pro and achieve currency trading success if you want to, it's up to you.

Trading Psychology - An Important Tip on How to Stay Focused While Trading

One of the most common questions is, "How can trading psychology help me to stay focused? I seem to easily become distracted and then miss good trades!"

The Dilemma

Many traders have the good intention of trading attentively, if not aggressively, and making money as soon as the market offers an opportunity. But the markets are not always willing to offer sound trades. Many times, the market will lock us out with a large directional move, or offer little profit due to a flat, range-bound day. How you respond to this can mean the difference between profit and loss.

Being Mindful

Everyone has lapses in concentration. This is just being human. It is, however, the high level performer that will recognize their lapse and immediately bring herself back into focus. This is the person we want to emulate.

A Way

In other words, if you were sitting next to an excellent trader and carefully observing her and what she does, what would you expect to see her do when she loses focus? Think carefully about this. Try to get into the mindset of the trader who exhibits a high level of excellence - someone you respect and would readily follow as a mentor.

The excellent trader will have lapses just like you and me (she is human too). What is different about the excellent trader? What makes her rise to the occasion when other 'would-bees' are still caught up in distracting activities? It's really not hard to discern. What would it take for you to pull yourself out of distraction and into focus?

Once you understand what that excellent trader would do when confronting a mental lapse, make these actions your personal 'model of action' that you strive for. The next time you notice you are distracted, engage your 'model of action' and gently bring yourself back to your market.

This is one useful response because it applies mindfulness to trading. Depending on personal characteristics and your individual situation, other considerations can be helpful. Nonetheless, this would be a very good start for most traders who struggle with the challenge of becoming distracted while trading.

Trading Psychology - Undo the Frustrations in Your Trading

Becoming frustrated challenges every trader. Trading psychology can help traders handle the many frustrations of trading. Feeling frustrated is just another way of saying that we don't like what the market is offering us. When things don't go our way, it's natural to get frustrated. But like so many things in life, it is how we respond to frustrating events that can make all the difference for a trader.

Let's look a little closer at how traders can become frustrated, and then look at a few constructive solutions.

How to get Frustrated Trading

Take every loss that occurs and personalize it: Be convinced that the swift market action against your position was done by "them," on purpose, just to catch your stop or shake you out. Be sure to let your mind run wild with thoughts about how you "always pick bad trades," and "always lose." Also, be sure to ask, "why does this always happen to me!"

Make trades outside of your trading plan: When the market starts to move, jump in, even though it's not a setup in your repertoire. But don't stop there! Keep trying new trading ideas when the setups in your plan either aren't triggering or have had 3-4 losses in a row. And, keep trying new indicators. Keep switching from the MACD to stochastics to RSI to CCI to adaptive moving averages and on and on.

Hold onto a bias: Come into the trading day knowing how the market is going to trade. Have the bias, for example, that the market is going to rally. Be sure to keep buying each new low as the market keeps falling, patting yourself on the back for picking each new bottom. Above all else, ignore the market action (and your mounting losses).

These may be a little overstated, but not by much. The point is that our mindset often makes us frustrated. We get into a vicious cycle where we are blaming and condemning, jumping from one thing to the next, or being stubborn in the face of contrary evidence. In the end, we only hurt ourselves.

How to undo the Frustration

Here are some ideas about choices we have in responding to events rather than being frustrated by them:

Reframe obstacles as learning opportunities: Start by accepting responsibility for losses. If you (not "they") are responsible, you can do something about them. Also, ask better questions. For example, "How can I learn from this experience so that I can improve my trading?" Look at losses as simply events, nothing more. Then, try to learn something new from each event that will benefit your trading in the future.

Work your trading plan: You put a lot of time and careful thought into your trading plan. Honor yourself and the work you did by committing to it and trading from it. Make it a personal goal to stop reacting to random market moves and start responding to the market through the principles and setups in your plan. When the market suddenly moves, refrain from reacting and jumping in. Instead, when the market offers you an opportunity consistent with your plan, you respond to that opportunity by taking the trade.

Anticipate: In your nightly analysis, consider how the market might trade the next day. Also consider the alternatives. You might assess the market as ready to rally. That's great. Also anticipate the alternatives. What would it look like if the market started to fall? What price levels would be breached that would tell you that? Now you are prepared for however the market might trade.

Trading Psychology: Developing the Trader's Mindset
Do you have the Trader's Mindset?

Developing a proper trading mindset is a must for trading success and can take some time. This is not an area where you can take a short cut. You develop the trader's mindset from actually trading and experiences you gain from trading, but the good news is that you can learn from other people's experiences and make them your own.

The Trader's Mindset will help you handle drawdowns, losses, and profits. Yes, profits can actually cause you stress!

Trading psychology is very powerful of which I am sure you have seen. If you show the same successful approach to one hundred different traders, no two of them will trade it exactly the same way.

Why is this you may ask? It is because each trader has a unique belief system, and their beliefs will determine their trading style. That is why even with a profitable and proven trading approach many traders will still fail.

They lack the proper belief system to enable them to trade well. In other words, they lack proper trading psychology.

Here is a list of some common psychological issues:

- Fear of being stopped out
- Fear of not taking enough profit
- Fear of being wrong
- Fear of success
- Analysis Paralysis

When you encounter psychological issues it is best to recognize the issue, be aware of it, and do not deny it. In order to fix psychological issues we as human beings must first become aware of the problem and issues in order to heal or fix the problem. This process can take years, because each individual must take responsibility for their problems to heal. Success in trading is a direct result of a sound trading system, sound money management, proper capitalization, and sound trading psychology.

These are by no means all the psychological issues but these are the most common. They usually center around the fact that for one reason or another, the trader is not following their chosen trading approach or system. And instead prefers to wing it or trade their emotions which in trading will always get you in trouble. So, I think you can see how psychology is all important in trading.

Our goal as traders in regards to psychology is to maintain an even keel so to speak when trading. Our winning trades and losing trades should not affect us. Obviously we are trading better when we are winning, but emotionally we should strive to maintain an even balance emotionally in regards to our wins and our losses.

It will happen when it happens and when you achieve this level of mental ability; it will come after working long and hard on your problems, but will come without you knowing it. It usually happens when you least expect it.

Below is a list of what one feels after acquiring the proper trader's mindset:

- Ability to focus on the present day
- Sense of calmness
- Aligning trades in the direction of the market
- Profits accumulating as your skills improve

- Learning from every trade
- A lot of enjoyment from trading

Trading your chosen approach or system and not being influenced by the market or others

When you can read the list above and genuinely say that's me, you have arrived!

Forex Trading Without Emotion

The finest, most profitable forex trading system is worthless in the hands of a trader that is filled with fear and emotion. Would you agree that this a bold statement? A beginner trader might think so. However, if you are an aspiring or experienced trader then you most likely have some idea of how true that statement is.

Many forex trading systems are sold without any regard to dealing with the fear and emotions that come along with trading the markets. I consider these systems sellers marketing incomplete strategies at the very least, and being unscrupulous at the very worst. To promote a forex trading system without teaching basic concepts in trading psychology says simply, "We don't care if you succeed in your trading endeavors but we would sure like your money for this sale!"

Lets define "trading psychology." Trading psychology, to me, is the field of study that includes all of the emotional aspects of financial trading that do not involve the trading system rules that you use to trade. Within this field fits all of the fear and emotion that a currency trader might feel when placing or exiting a trade. Adequately dealing with this fear and emotion is the difference between success and failure in the forex trading business.

Why, if working positively with the fears and emotions of trading is paramount to being a profitable trader, is the subject so commonly not dealt with adequately? Understanding trading psychology is not required in order to purchase a trading system, so the seller has no vested interest in disclosing these required skills to the buyer. A sellers goal is to sell, not to educate, train, or enlighten.

It is of utmost importance that traders can and should elevate their understanding of trading psychology by searching out and performing simple trading exercises that can dramatically affect (positively) their mindset, their enjoyment of trading, and their profitability.

Awareness is the first step in recognizing the need for a trading psychology plan. Novice traders must realize and embrace that the mental part of the trading game is a normal and real stumbling block to achieving success. At one point or another, every trader must raise the white flag and realize that there are powerful mental forces that may be preventing from being successful in the forex market.

Now that we recognize the absolute need for a trading psychology plan in order to be a consistently profitable trader, we can set some goals.

- ☐   I will always adhere to my entry rules.
- ☐   If I miss my entry, I will wait until the next setup
- ☐   I will manage my trades by my exit rules and not by guessing the market's moves
- ☐   I will not trade based on feel, only on what I see
- ☐   I will not trade with emotion or fear.
- ☐   I will not take more risk than my trading plan allows

Goals will get you started on your way toward understanding your mental trading challenges.

We have recognized the importance of trading psychology and developed some goals to accomplish on our way to taking the fear and emotion out of our trading. Where do we go from here? One of the easiest ways to get started on your journey to accomplishing your trading psychology goals is to design a strict, live trading regimen that forces you to stick to your rules and trading plan without fail. In other words, practice your system "perfectly" for at least 100 trades. As we practice, we will need to record every trade we take (entry, exit, time, result). Trade with real money and trade microlots, or $.01 per pip.

By practicing perfectly, you will gradually start to feel the stress leave your trading and the fear that is associated with losing a trade begin to subside. Repeat this process until your trading rules become second nature and, win or lose, you feel the same at the end of the trading day.

Understanding and recognizing the role that psychology plays in your trading is an absolute must in developing trading success. Facing the mental challenges of trading head on will not only allow you to become a profitable trader, it will also make your trading experience much more enjoyable. Once this realization is made, write down some goals and focus on the things that will give you a starting point in dealing with the fear and emotion in trading the markets.

Practicing and recording 100s of trades on a small live trading account are your first steps toward managing your fears and trading successfully without emotion. If you will follow these simple steps, you will be well on your way to being part of the 5% of traders that are consistently profitable.

Forex trading should not be (but can be) an over complex adventure. Big Brain Forex is your source for a simple and elegant trading strategy that can be used to make strong consistent gains in the forex market.

Simplicity in concept, ease of execution and commitment to your consistent profitability make Big Brain Forex a unique and honest proposition in an industry that is replete with charlatans.

CHAPTER 7
Day Trading Strategies

Day trading is defined as the process of purchasing and selling securities all within the course of a trading day. Traders buy securities, whether stocks, bonds, or futures, and then sell them before the end of the day. Day traders never hold positions overnight. The reason is that they fear overnight activity could harm their positions and hence the need to terminate positions by the close of the trading day.

After Hours Trading

The equities markets in the United States usually close down at 4.00 pm eastern time. Even then, traders continue to have access to the markets until 8.00 pm in the night. Access is enabled via platforms such as ECN and exchanges such as the NYSE. Therefore, trading the markets any time after 4.00 pm till 8.00 pm in the night is referred to as after-hours trading, post-market trading, or extended hours trading. The problem with this trading period is that it is very illiquid as most trading specialists and market makers avoid trading at these times.

The most outstanding feature of after-hours trading is the lack of liquidity in the market. A lot of experts consider this to be risky or even dangerous territory because there is often very little activity. Spreads are often very wide as most of the other traders, especially market makers, have left for the day. Therefore, the securities' activity is often very low. However, day traders know how to benefit from such situations. For instance, if breaking news is announced during this period, then related stocks could have significant action that can be traded.

Trading after hours is tricky due to the illiquid nature of most securities as well as the large spreads. The best time to trade after hours is only when there is a significant news item that affects a particular company or an industry. Such news is best if received during the earnings periods, which occur mostly during quarterly earnings reporting times. This kind of trading should, therefore, be left to seasoned traders only.

High-Frequency Trading

High-frequency trading, also referred to as HFT, are essentially programs that execute complex algorithms that can generate superfast trades across different markets. The purpose of these rapid trades includes arbitrage and market making. The outstanding feature here is the thin profits that accrue from the large volumes of trades initiated. Trades initiated can number in their millions on any given day. It is said that about 50% or half of the volume trades initiated in US stock markets are HFT.

These trades rarely hold a position for long. One of the most useful ingredients in any HFT operation is low latency in order to keep the speed advantage over other traders such as retail traders. It is a modern computer algorithm that power HFTs. If well executed, such programs can generate modest to average profits for a long period of time without incurring any significant losses. There are reports of HFT firms of running for 1000 profitable days without any losses. When everything works as required, then HFT offers a great opportunity to earn plenty of money with very little risk over a long period of time.

Latency: This term actually refers to the time taken for data transmitted between two points to get to its destination. Basically, low latency refers to high speeds, while high latency means low speeds. Most investment companies invest a lot of resources in acquiring the latest, cutting edge infrastructure and hardware necessary for processing trades at high speeds.

Algorithms: These are basically instructions set out which are to be executed once certain conditions are met. A sophisticated algorithm such as the HFC algorithm used in trade has millions of lines of code. In recent years, algorithms have become commonplace, and most traders make use of one type or another to execute their trades.

Momentum Trading

Day traders choose momentum trading simply because all the action is on the stock market momentum. This type of day trading aims at profiting from stocks that experience a price gain, especially with huge trade volumes. In momentum trading, stocks and securities are affected by factors such as margin calls, short squeezes, and stop losses, so they move in an excessive and extreme manner. The typical approach by day traders on momentum trading is to scalp profits as quickly as possible and with as much leverage as possible.

Day traders who prefer momentum trading usually trade any security that has large volatility and significant volume. These include securities that have sustained a significant rise in price and are known as high-flyers or momentum stocks. Most of the stocks suitable for this kind of trade strategy are more volatile than those of major blue chip companies. It is this volatility that attracts momentum traders to these trades. Volatility provides a great option to capitalize and benefit from price movements and volume. Securities with large volumes and high volatility that feature in the news are usually the best suited to momentum trading.

Price movement: This is the hallmark of momentum day trading. Traders often make use of shorter time frame charts like the 15-minute, 5-minute, and even the 1-minute charts. In order to manage risk, the focus should be on the immediate action with large share volumes. It is important for momentum day traders to have precision when entering and leaving the market.

Executions and charts will, in this case, carry significantly more weight compared to the fundamentals of the underlying company. Also, stories in the news carry more weight as news is often the main driver of momentum. Also, chart patterns and essential signals will help determine the best times to initiate trades.

Things momentum traders should look out for

- High probability chart patterns
- Intraday setups
- Volume
- The reasonable risk to reward ratios

Options Day Trading

A stock option is yet another trading option commonly used by day traders. Options contracts ideally offer the holder a right with no obligation to sell or purchase an underlying security at a certain price. Options actually are derivatives. This means that their price is derived from an underlying security or even commodity. Therefore, like other derivatives, stock options enable the holder to enjoy the benefits of the price movement of the underlying security, yet the losses they can incur are capped on the option.

A stock options trader basically enjoys the benefits of stock ownership without the obligation or financial implication of having to buy the stock. They only incur costs that are a fraction of the total cost of buying or investing in the stock. Each and every options contract has about 100 shares of the underlying security attached to it. So a trader holding 10 call or put options basically has control of 1000 shares of the underlying stock.

Many exchanges accept and trade in options contracts. These include exchanges such as the International Securities Exchange, Chicago Boards Options, and many others. This is also due to the fact that their prices move up and down in tandem with the underlying stock. However, options are unlike stocks because they can lose most of their value should their time expire. All options come with an expiry date as this is an inherent aspect they all possess.

Penny Stocks Trading

What are penny stocks? These are stocks trading on the markets that are worth less than $5 each. They constitute some of the most speculative shares in the market, and most of the times are priced at less than $3 and even $1. There is always the concern about fraud, speculation, and even pump and dump tendencies. However, things have improved and so penny stocks are now viewed as a less expensive option for investing in stocks at the markets.

The essential ingredients when trading penny stocks are volumes and liquidity. These two ingredients make it easy to enter and exit trades. It is also essential that any day trader dealing in penny stocks have direct access to a brokerage to execute any trades fast and seamlessly. Penny stocks have a tendency of increased volumes then peaking eventually and leaving plenty of traders trapped with expensive shares. Before entering such trades, it is important to perform exhaustive research and make use of all tools and leverage in order to have the best information possible. With penny stocks, the essential point to remember is that price is key so always have an exit plan way before commencing any trade.

Pre-market Trading

Another type of day trading strategy is pre-market trading. Trading in these markets begins as early as 4.00 am EST even though the normal pre-market trading hours start at 8.00 am EST. It is during the normal trading hours that liquidity and high volumes begin to stream in. regular trading starts at 09.30 am EST.

Pre-market trading is generally accessible via dark pools and ECNs. This is very similar to after-hours trading. While there are generally no specialists or market makers in the market at such hours, it is possible that they may be participating in the markets via certain ECNs.

Pre-market trading versus after hours

Generally, the risks of trading the pre-market are much lower compared to the after-hours session. This is because action continues within the markets after 09.30 am EST as compared to after-hours where activity just shuts off. Many traders are likely to be trapped in after-hours trading because it ends at 8.00 pm. Such traders will have no option but to wait until pre-market hours the following morning. Also, trade can resume with a sharp gap against positions taken by the traders.

My Strategies

In this chapter, I will be getting you familiar with some of my bestkown strategies, based on three key elements: (1) the price action, (2) the technical indicators, and (3) the candlesticks and chart patterns. It is of upmost important to learn and practice these three elements simultaneously. However, some strategies only require the application of the technical indicators (which includes the moving averages and VWAP), it is quite helpful to have a perfect knowledge of the price action and chart patterns to ensuring one become a successful day trader. This market knowlegde, most especially the price action, often comes as a result of constant practice and experience. As a day trader, you should never be bothered about the earnings of companies. The actions and earnings of companies should not be a thing of concern to Day traders. As a day trade your sole attention and interest should only be drawn to these elements which are the price action, chart patterns and technical indicators. Over my years of practice and experience I have come to know more stock symbols than the real names of companies. I have always ensure i never mingle fundamental analysis with technical analysis while taking a trade; I basically focus solely on the technical indicators. As a short-term investor I am not drawn to the the fundamental aspects of companiesI don't care – this is one of my qualities as a day trader. We trade very fast - guerrilla trading! – depending on the trade, some period could be has short as ten to thirty seconds. Every trader is required to understand a particular strategy and edge that works best for them. Each trader needs to be able to identify a particular spot in the market where they feel really comfortable to trade. Over my trading years, I have focused on these particular strategies because they seems to work quite fine for me. I have also recognized that the best setups are these strategies and I will be diving indepth to explaining them in this chapter. These element in theory,seems simple, but they are however difficult to master and usually require plenty of practice. These trading strategies will provide the needed signals relatively infrequently and enusre you have the perfect point of entry into the market especially during the quiet times, just like professionals do. Also, always take note of the fact that in the market right now, more than 60% of the volume are algorithmic high frequency trading. This means that as a trader you are always against computers.

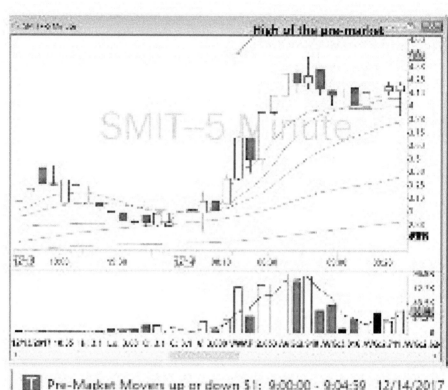

High of the pre-market

SMIT--5 Minute

Symbol	$	T	C $	C %	Float		Spread
SMIT	4.14	679,647	1.69	69.2	2,771,480	0.15	0.06
MBOT	7.16	452,836	0.14	13.7	25.01M	0.05	15.16
SRAX	5.77	151,271	0.67	13.1	6,284,760	1.16	16.32
PSDV	1.22	75,630	0.07	6.1	45.20M	0.07	2.44
AMPE	1.84	762,114	0.09	5.1	66.15M	0.25	11.01
OPW	5.20	435,585	0.15	3.0	6,065,340	1.24	10.40
HMNY	6.96	153,663	0.16	2.4	5,864,440	1.67	
UGAZ	5.72	1.43M	-0.12	-2.1		0.84	
AU	9.00	112,366	-0.43	-4.6	407.00M	0.32	
PTI	5.04	1.10M	-0.43	-7.9	21.15M	0.65	4.53
SBGL	4.37	344,393	-0.63	-12.5	286.36M	0.22	
PIR	4.26	341,748	-1.58	-27.1	80.61M	0.25	12.36

If you are used to playing the game of chess against computers, you wil know from such that you are most likely going to lose but however, you might get lucky a couple of times, but if you keep on playing often and you are most likely guaranted to lose. This same rule is applicable to algorithmic trading. Day traders are always trading stocks against computer systems. However, on the one hand, this represents a problem. What this could only mean is that the majority of variations and changes in stocks that you see are obviously as a result of the computer system moving shares around. However, this means that there are only a few handful of stocks each day that are often traded on a very heavy retail volume (as opposed to institutional algorithmic trading) that you can overpower the algorithmic trading and you and I, who are the retail traders, will control that stock. Every other day, as a retail trader you will need to pay close attention to trading those particular stocks. These are some of the strategies I will discuss in Chapter 3 which is the Stock in Play, these are stocks that are typically gapping up or down on earnings.

You must ensure you spot stocks that have significant retail traders' interest and with significant retail volume. These will be the stocks to trade, and collectively, we the people, the retail traders, will get to overpower the computers. Personally, I make use of candlestick charts which I explained in Chapter 5. A candlestick on its own represents a period of time. As I have previously mentioned, one can always choose any intraday time-frame, which is often dependent on the personality of the trader and trading technique. This candlestick timeframe includes: the hourly charts, 5-minute charts, or even 1-minute charts. Personally for me, my preference is always 5-minute charts, but I do closely monitor the 1-minute charts. Always remember and pay attention that one of the most reliable philosophy of trading is that you must master and practice only a few solid setups to be consistently profitable. Without doubt, creating a very simple trading strategy will help in reducing confusion as well as stress and allow you to concentrate more on the psychological aspect of trading. This is what often defines winners from losers.

Strategy 1:
The Fallen Angel is one of the most important trading strategy that I use for low float stocks which is often referred to as the "Fallen Angel". An Angel is a low float stock (which is less than twenty million shares) that has gapped up noticeably due to the level of importance of fundamental news. These stocks are usually traded heavily in the pre-market, with more than one million shares before the market opens. When there are low float stocks, and for this particular strategy, the volume of trade is often the key. However,If those stocks do not have much volume, irregardless of how much it has gapped up, or what the stock float is, you are advised to always try to stay away from it. The Low volume low float stocks are usually subjected to "pump and dump" or manipulation and

trading them sometimes may results in heavy losses. The Angel (our low float Stock in Play) usually get to open higher and makes a recent high of the day quickly, but usually before the end of the day will then sell off heavily. This first uptick at the Open of trade is often more likened trap for bullish traders, and is usually followed by a massive sell off which is either caused as a result of heavy profit taking from overnight traders or the actions of short sellers or in some cases both. When the Angel sells off, it also has every right to fall, however, if it holds a support, it usually comes back up above VWAP and the previous high of the day. That's typically when you want to catch it. To summarize this pattern: when the market opens, the stock will make a recent high of the day but will sell off very quick. You do not want to jump into the trade yet, not until it consolidates around a trading level such as the low of the pre-market, or moving averages on a daily or 5-minute chart. As soon as the stock is experiencing an uptrend with heavy volume, that is the right moment to take the trade to the long side. The entry sign into the market is to see a new 1- minute or 5-minute high after the consolidation with MASSIVE volume only. You have to remember that the volume on the way up needs to be significantly higher than that of the previous candlesticks. To illustrate this strategy, I will be reviewing my Gappers watchlist on the 14th of December, 2017, as it is shown in Figure 1. As you will see, Schmitt Industries, Inc. (ticker: SMIT) gapped up almost 70% with heavy volume at the pre-market. From my watchlist you will see that, by 9 a.m. almost 700,000 shares have been traded. You will also notice that SMIT is a low float stock with a float of only 2.7 million shares. For your perusal, I have also included in Figure 1 a 5-minute chart for SMIT showing its pre-market activity.

High of the pre-market

SMIT--5 Minute

Symbol	S	T	C $	C %	Rel		
SMIT	4.14	679,647	1.69	69.2	2,771,480	0.15	0.06
MIKI	1.16	452,806	0.14	13.7	25.01M	0.05	15.16
SRAX	5.77	151,271	0.67	13.1	6,284,760	1.16	16.32
PSDV	1.22	75,630	0.07	6.1	45.20M	0.07	2.44
AMPE	1.84	762,114	0.09	5.1	66.15M	0.25	11.01
OPW	5.20	435,585	0.15	3.0	6,065,340	1.24	10.40
HMNY	6.95	153,663	0.16	2.4	5,364,440	1.67	5.41
UGAZ	5.72	1.43M	-0.12	-2.1		0.84	
AU	0.00	112,366	-0.43	-4.5	407.00M	0.32	
PTI	5.04	1.10M	-0.43	-7.9	21.15M	0.65	4.53
SBGL	4.37	344,393	-0.63	-12.6	236.36M	0.22	
PIR	4.26	341,748	-1.58	-27.1	80.61M	0.25	12.36

Figure 2 – Shows my Gappers watchlist on the 14th of December, 2017 (bottom) and 5-minute chart showing the pre-market activity of SMIT (top). you will notice that in Figure 2, at the Open SMIT went higher and quickly to a price of $4.36 but then had a quick sell off below VWAP to a price of $3.70 and held that level for about 30 minutes. Right after 10 a.m., SMIT made a new 5-minute and 1-minute high (when compared to previous candles) with heavy volume and moved toward the VWAP. It pushed toward the previous high of the day at a price of $4.36 and eventually toward the high of the pre-market when the price was at $4.48. A great point of entry would have been around 10:05 a.m. when the market price was at $3.80 when SMIT made a 1-minute high above the 9 and 20 EMA with a stop loss below $3.70 (all shown in Figure 2). As discussed, the profit target could have been the VWAP at around $4, the previous high of the day with price at $4.36, and the high of the pre-market at $4.48.

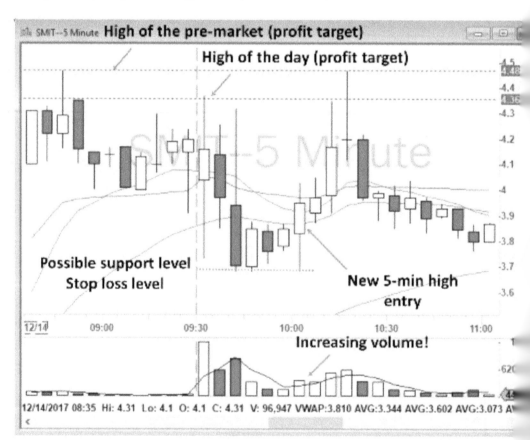

In Figure 3 and 4 - Shows the 5-minute and 1-minute charts of SMIT with the potential point of entry into the trade, exit and stop loss levels.

As you can deduced, I have always preached and practiced my strategies, I did trade SMIT on that day which is based on this strategy and quite rewarding with an amazing profit of $883, clearly in Figure 5. I also did trade other stocks which are really not relevant to this strategy.

Symb	Realized	Type	Company Name
FNSR	511.41	Short	Finisar Corporation - (
SMIT	883.12	Margin	Schmitt Industries, Inc
TEVA	-70.68	Short	Teva Pharmaceutical
VRX	93.75	Short	Valeant Pharmaceutic
VRX	552.86	Margin	Valeant Pharmaceutic
Summary	**1970.46**		

Figure 5 – Shows my closed P&L on the 14th day of December, 2017.
Another illustration can be seen in my trading of Genocea Biosciences, Inc. (ticker: GNCA) after its surprisingly brilliant and rewarding earnings on Friday, the 21st of July, 2017. As soon as the market opened on Monday, the 24th of July,

the price of GNCA was at $5.70, but it expreienced a downward trend and quickly finished off selling at $5.30 to consolidate at that level. You will notice that in Figure 6.4, that both the 50 SMA which appears on my 5-minute chart and the 200 SMA which also appeared on my 1-minute chart at $5.30. When both the moving average are on the 5-minute and 1-minute charts, this tends to make the level even more stronger. The GNCA consolidated between prices at $5.40 to $5.30 until a 1-minute high was achieved at about 9:47 a.m with the heavy volume toward the previous high of the day at the price of $5.70 and the high of the pre-market at the price of $5.75. After the high of the pre-market has been tested with price at $5.75, it however sold off back toward the low of the day. A good entry into market would definitely have been at the price of $5.40 with the stop loss below $5.30 and profit targets at price of $5.70 and $5.75.

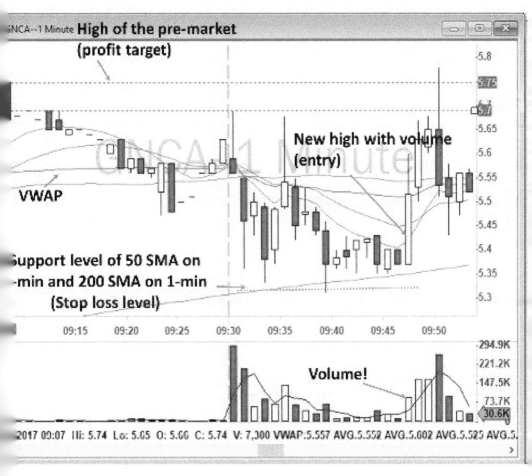

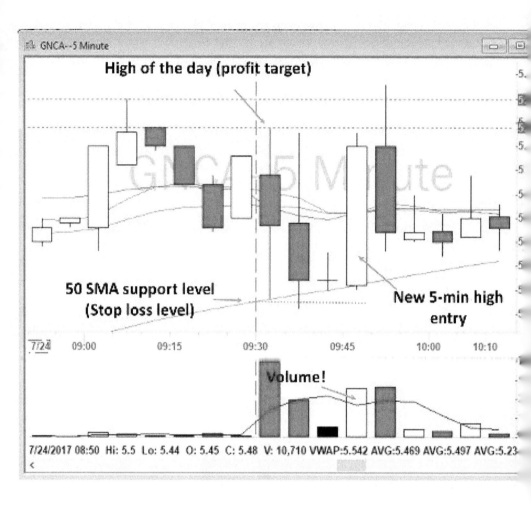

Figure 6 and 7 – Shows the 5-minute and 1-minute charts of GNCA shows the market potential entry point, it exit and stop loss levels.

I was quite able to take this trade, but I was not fortunate enough to make a perfect entry into the market. I had an entry point with price at $5.55, I added more shares when the price was at $5.60, and exit with sell when price was at $5.75, making a profit of just $325, as it is shown, along with my point of entries and exits from the market, in Figure 8. You should always note that the window to make a perfect entry into the market is always short and trades happen quickly, thereby making the perfect entry and proper exit very difficult.

63

Symb	Realized	Type	Company N
APRN	120.20	Short	Blue Apron H
DRYS	229.06	Margin	DryShips Inc
GNCA	325	Margin	Genocea Bio
HIBB	0	Short	Hibbett Spor
DRYS	205.89	Margin	DryShips Inc
Summary	**880.15**		

Market Clock

07/24/17 10:52:08

In Figure 8 and 9 above — This shows the Screenshot of my real time trade on GNCA which is on a 5-minute chart on the 24th of July, 2017 with my points of entries and exits and the screenshot of my closed P&L for the day. However, Similar trading behavior were noticeable on the GNCA the next day. In Figure 10, which happens to be my Top List for the 25th of July, 2017, shows that GNCA was still one of the Nasdaq's most active and highest gainers. After a fundamental news break, Stocks in Play remained in play for a few days.

Nasdaq Active

Nasdaq Gainer

Top List

	NASAc...	NASG...	NASL...	LSTAct...	LSTG...
1	MU	FLKS	CUR	BAC	IVC
2	AMD	ASPS	NVAX	FCX	SRCI
3	DCIX	MBRX	STX	VALE	AKS
4	NVAX	NLST	PCRX	XLF	FCX
5	STX	IDRA	ASTE	AKS	SALT
6	TOPS	SMRT	HSTM	SPY	BKS
7	DCTH	GNCA	DRYS	VXX	ATI
8	QQQ	SGMS	LOGI	EEM	GUSH
9	AAPL	MRNS	SANM	C	HBM
10	DRYS	ASNA	LECO	GE	SVU
11	SRPT	PDCE	AGEN	TRQ	CRC
12	FB	HIBB	IONS	F	NEM
13	HBAN	HDP	MBVX	CHK	DDS
14	MSFT	MYOK	XGTI	BTI	MC
15	NVDA	TNTR	RWLK	VALE.P	TGB
16	INTC	AREX	VRAY	IPG	CBI
17	GNCA	WWD	ABEO	USO	CRR

Market Clock

07/25/17 10:43:47

Figure 10 – My Top List on the 25th of July, 2017.

From Figure 11 you can see that, as at the time the market opened around 9:30 a.m on the 25th of July, 2017, GNCA was on a uptrend to make the high of the day when price was at $6.55, but then went ahead to sell quickly making the price of $6.20 and consolidated at that level. Noticeably, as at the day before, the 50 SMA on my 5-minute chart was trending around this consolidation area, at this time the price was at $6.20. The GNCA consolidated between $6.20 to $6.30 until it was able to make a new 1-minute high at 9:43 a.m which was toward the previous high of the day when price was at $6.55 and the high of the pre-market with the price of $6.69. GNCA further went above the price of $6.79 before it finally could sell off back toward its low of the day. The perfect point of entry would have been when the price was around $6.35 with a stop loss placed just directly below $6.30 and profit target at $6.55 and $6.69.

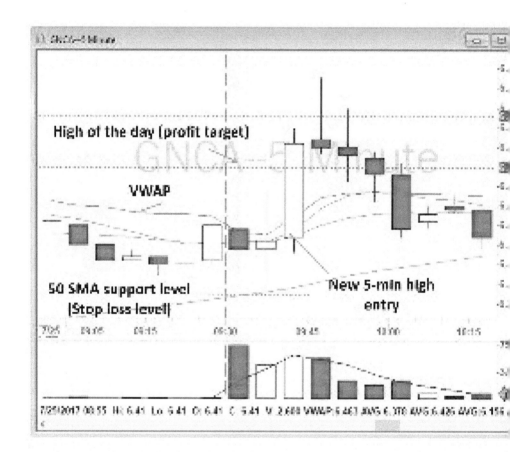

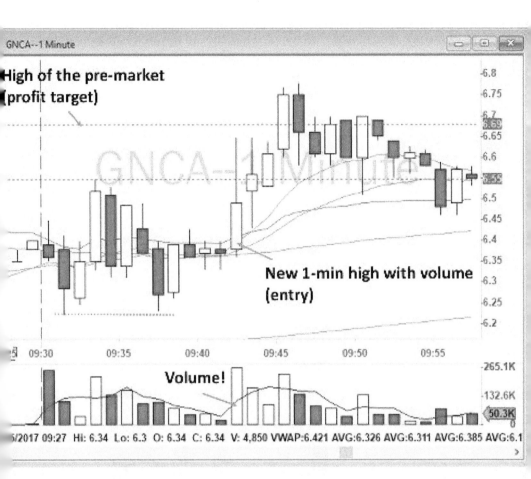

Figures 11 and 12 – This shows the 1-minute and 5-minute charts of GNCA on the 25th of July, 2017 with the potential point of entry, exit and stop loss levels. This is another illustration of the Fallen Angel Strategy which can be seen when DryShips Inc. (ticker: DRYS) experienced another wild day of trading after its one-for-seven reverse stock split. The market on the 24th of July, 2017 opened at 9:30 a.m and DRYS had an upttrend and the price was at $2.75, but also went ahead to sell off quickly making the price of $2.35 and consolidated around that level. In the Figure 12, it can be seen that, both the 200 SMA on my 1-minute and 50 SMA appeared on my 5-minute chart were also seen to make a price around this $2.35 level. As I have previously mentioned, having this two important moving averages both on the 1-minute and the 5-minute charts will provide strength and make the level way stronger. DRYS consolidated between the price of $2.45 to $2.30 until it was able to make a new 5-minute high as at 9:57 a.m. with heavy volume trending toward the previous high of the day with

67

the price was at $2.75 and the high of the pre-market making $2.84. After the high of the pre-market was challenged, it also moved toward testing yesterday's pre- market high at $2.95, before it finally sold off falling back below the VWAP. The perfect point of maket entry would have been when it made the price of $2.45 with it stop loss just below $2.30 and it target profit at $2.75, $2.84, and $2.95.

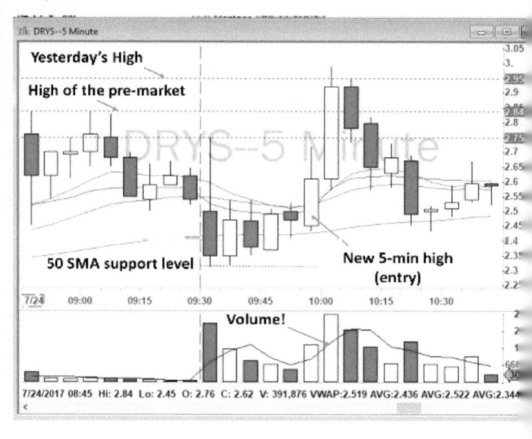

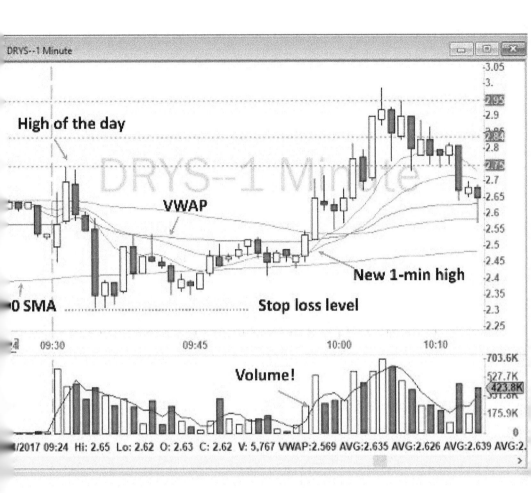

Figure 13 and 14 – My 5-minute and 1-minute charts of DRYS on 24th of July, 2017, it shows a potential point of market entry, it exit and stop loss levels.

This example of the Fallen Angel Strategy can be seen on Capricor Therapeutics Inc. (ticker: CAPR) on the 27th of July, 2017, as it was set out in Figure 15. The market opened at 9:30 a.m., CAPR had an uptrend and price quickly went up to $1.56, but then had to sell off quickly toward the low of the pre-market when the price was at around $1.30 to $1.35 and consolidated around that level. After it consolidation, the market experienced a new 5-minute high and also a new 1-minute high at 9:45 a.m. with this heavy volume trending toward the previous high of the day with price at $1.56 and the high of the pre-market with price at $1.63. After the high of the pre-market was also challenged, it then took a sell off back below the VWAP at around 10:05 a.m. The perfect point of entry into this market would have been when the price was around $1.40 with a stop loss

69

placed just below the price of $1.30 and profit targets when the price was at $1.56 and $1.63 are met (a risk/reward ratio of approximately 2).

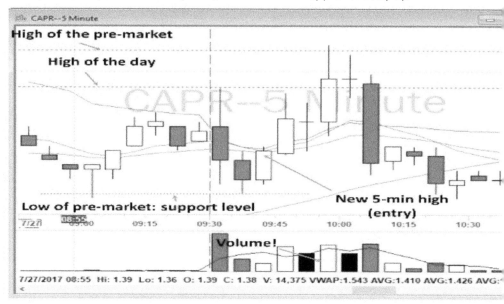

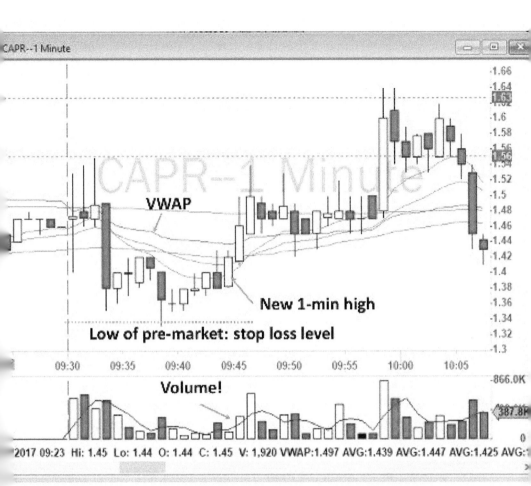

Figure 15 and 16 – The 1-minute and 5-minute charts of CAPR on the 27th of July, 2017 which shows the potential point of entry into the market, it exit and stop loss levels.

Summarizing this strategy:

An Angel is a low float Stock in Play which is gapping with heavy volume in the pre-market. At the time of the market Opening, our Angel makes a recent high of the day but however sold off very fast. Jumping on such a trade would not be advisable at least not until the market consolidates around an important trading level such as the low of the pre-market, or the moving averages on your daily or 5-minute chart. This will be the point where our Angel will have fall to. But as soon as you see the stocks coming back up with heavy volume, this will be the perfect timing to take your trade to the long side. The signal for market entry is to see a new 1-minute or 5-minute high after the consolidation with MASSIVE volume only. You should always pay close attention to the volume, in cases like this, you must always remember that the volume on the way up must be significantly higher than that of the previous candles. The stop loss is usually just below the consolidation period. The profit target can be placed at (1) VWAP, (2) the previous high of the day, (3) the high of the pre-market, and (4) any other important level nearby such as Y High or Y Low. It is often advisable to always fall back to an obvious support level and consolidation before entering a trade. If you can not find one, it is advised not to trade the stock. Whenever you see a breakout but not with a strong volume, it is also advised to rather not trade such stock. Trading with Fallen Angel is generally a difficult strategy, the level of risk in fallen angel is so difficult to manage. From the previous examples above, you must have noticed the drops that occurred, they are quite sharp and comes with certain level of risks. If you are not quick enough to pull out of a losing trade, you might get stucked in a very bad position and be forced to accept a heavy loss of capital. The gapping of stocks do come significantly and can also lose this gap during the day, so trying to hold them during the day might not be the best of ideas, especially if the volume is droping during the day. It is recommended that new day trader pratice this strategy with simulator for some period of time to gain expereince before attempting to trade live. However, even at that when you go live always remember to take a significantly small percentage of your capital in order to minimise the level of risk. I know, it really seems like it is easy to take a 10,000 share on a $1 stock, but always remember, that every cent up and down in a $1 stock is the equivalent of a 1% swing in your position. One of my money management strategies is usually to take 4,000 shares for low float stocks below $10.

Strategy 2:

ABCD Pattern / Reverse ABCD Pattern The ABCD Pattern is one of the most fundamental and easiest patterns to trade with, and it has been proven to be a rewarding and an excellent choice for beginners and intermediate day traders. Although, this strategy might seem quite basic and simple and has been known for a very long time,but it still works effectively and efficiently, because of this so many traders even the professionals still make use of this trading stratregy. As a trader you should try to pay attention to the actions of other, you should do whatever they do because being on a trend is an important factor to being a successful trader, the trend is your friend. In fact, a trend may very well be your only friend in the market. Let us take a look at this pattern in Figure 17:

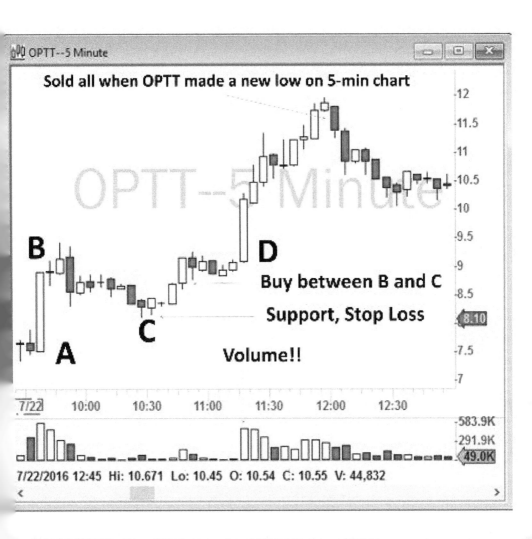

Figure 17 – This is an illustration of an ABCD Pattern on OPTT.

ABCD Patterns start with a strong uptrend movement. Buyers are aggressively incharge of the market, buying stocks from point A and making constantly recent highs of the day (at point B). You would want to enter the trade, but you should never chase it, because at point B with the recent highs it becomes extended and already with a high price. In addition, you cannot perfectly establish where your stop loss should be placed. Also, please do note that you must never take a trade without knowing where your stop loss would be placed. At point D, the traders who were fortunate enough to buy the stock earlier start selling slowly for profit, this action of the trader will affect the stock and the price will start to gradually fall. As soon as the actions of this trader starts reflecting on the market and the price of the stock starts falling, you should still not enter the trade or jump on

73

the downward trend because you do not know where the bottom of this pull back will be. However, if you can establish that the price does not fall from a certain level, just as point C, this could only mean one thing, that the stock has found a potential support level. Therefore, you have a clean shot and a potential point of entry into the market and can plan your trade and set up stop loss and a profit taking point, so take the shot. The screenshot above, which is labelled as Figure 6.10, is of Ocean Power Technologies, Inc. (ticker: OPTT) at the 22nd of July, 2016, when they made an announcement of a new $50 million contract to build a new ship (there's a fundamental catalyst! Remember Chapter 3?). The stock upsurged up from $7.70 (A) to $9.40 (B) at around 9:40 a.m. I could not make the first push higher as well as so many other traders, but had to watch and study the market to wait for point B, and a confirmation that the stock was not going to sell lower than a certain price (at point C). After I have reliased that point C was going to be a support as it held the price from falling further down and that buyers would not let the stock price go any lower than $8.10 (at point C), I entered the trade and bought 1,000 shares of OPTT near point C, with my stop loss being a break below point C. I have always known that as soon as the stock price go higher, closer to point B, traders who are willing to buy will jump on the trade massively. As I have mentioned previously, the ABCD Pattern is a very classic strategy and many retail traders look for it. Looking at point D, you will realise that there is a sudden spike in the volume of stocks traded, this could only mean that more traders were coming into the market to trade. My profit target was placed at a point when the stock made a new low on a 5-minute chart, which was a sign of weakness. Form Figure 17 you can see that, OPTT had a great run up when the price was at $12 and showed weakness by making a new low on a 5-minute chart when the price was at $11.60. That was the point I had to sell off all of my position. Figure 18 is also an illustration, this time for SPU on the 29th of August, 2016. This example shows the application of two ABCD Patterns. I marked out the second one as abcd pattern. Usually, as the trading day progresses, the volume of stocks tends to become lower and therefore the second pattern was smaller in size. You should always note that you are most likely to have higher volumes at point B and D (and in this instance also at points b and d).

Figure 18 – Shows an Example of ABCD Pattern and abcd pattern on SPU.

The next example, as it shown in Figure 19, is for Advanced Micro Devices, Inc. (ticker: AMD) on the 24th of July, 2017. At the Open, AMD had a price upsurge from $14 to $14.21 and did sold off back to the VWAP. For about 10 minutes, it consolidated above the VWAP and again experienced an upward trend of price as it moved higher toward the previous high of the day at $14.21 and further to the daily level at $14.42. The perfect point of market entry would be identified from my 1-minute chart when the stock found a support level at VWAP and then moved toward point B which is higher than the previous candle volume. However, the stop loss could have been a break just below VWAP and the daily level of price at $14.42 would have been a reasonable profit target.

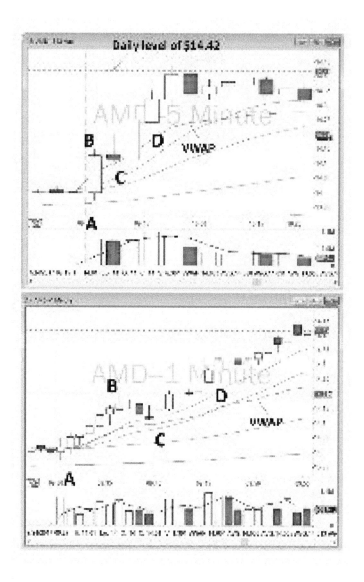

Figure 19 – This shows an Example of ABCD Pattern on AMD.

The following example, which is set out in Figure 20, is for Micron Technology, Inc. (ticker: MU) on 12th of March, 2018. If you take a look at the 5-minute chart (which is the top image), you would see that at the opening of the trade, MU moved from an initial price of $56.38 (at point A) to $57.75 (at point B) and finaly sold off back to the VWAP for about 15 minutes. It consolidated above the VWAP (at point C) and again experience an uptrend higher toward the previous high of the day with the price at $57.75. A perfect point of entry on the 5-minute chart would be when MU made a new 5-minute high above VWAP, as marked in the top image. I personally took this trade earlier in the day, just when another ABCD

Pattern had appeared on my 1-minute chart. This example will show you the several patterns of ABCD on the 5-minute and 1-minute charts. I have been able to mark out two patterns on the 1-minute chart and one on the 5-minute charts. The point of entry which I have marked on the 5-minute chart is exactly the same as the entry point I marked out as the second ABCD Pattern on the 1-minute chart.

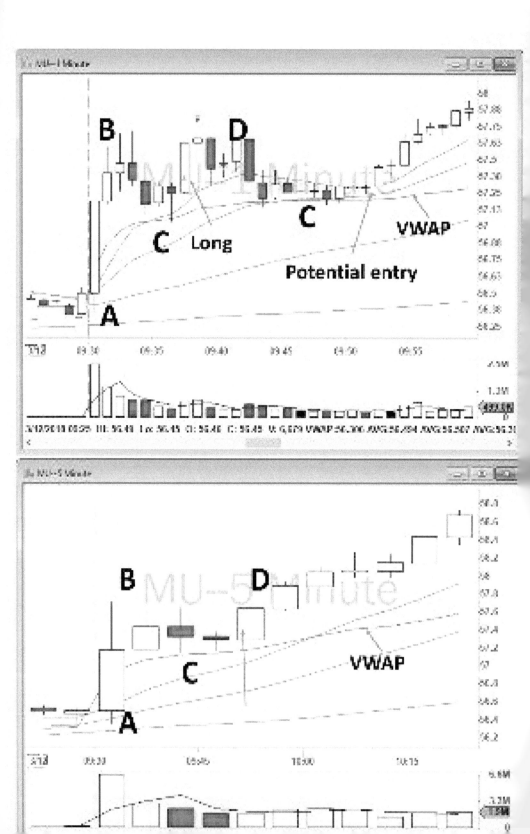

Figure 20 – Shows an Example of ABCD Patterns on MU as set out on the 1-minute chart, where the stock found a support at VWAP and took an upward trend toward point B with high volume (which is significantly higher than those of the previous candle volume), I went along with the trend and decided to sell toward the high of the day. My initial stop loss was a break below the VWAP when the price was at $57.13. Just after I did sold off some of my position, I had to adjust my stop loss to the break-even point and then eventually pulled out at the break-even position. However, I was not able to make a large profit on this trade as I only sold off just 25% of my position and then had to pull out of the remaining 75% of my position at the point when my trade was at break-even. Figure 21 is a screenshot of my P&L.

Symb	Realized	Type	Company Name
MU	225.84	Margin	Micron Technolog
QD	426.81	Margin	Qudian Inc. Amer
QD	165.52	Short	Qudian Inc. Amer
Summary	818.17		

Market Clock

03/12/18 10:11:51

Figure 21 – Shows my my P&L on MU.
This is an example of Another excellent ABCD Pattern on NXT-ID Inc. (ticker: NXTD) which occurred on the 21st of December, 2017, as it can be seen in Figure

22. Taking a look at the 5-minute chart (which is on the top image), it can be seen that at the Open, NXTD had an upward trend from when the price was at $4 (at point A) to a price of $6.74 (at point B) and eventually sold off back to the VWAP (at point C) at around 10:15 a.m. For the duration of about 20 minutes, it consolidated above the VWAP and then it had an upward movement toward the previous high of the day when the price was at $6.74. it however further went long towards point D when the price was at $6.50 and finally had a sell toward the high of the day with the price at $7. Meanwhile, a better entry to the market would have been to enter early. If I had paid close attention to the 1-minute chart, I could have easily read this. As you would notice, I went long too late, just before the break of the high of the day, but the point where the price was at $6.25 would have been a much prefred and better market entry. To determine a better position to place your stop loss, taking a close evaluation of the 1-minute chart will be of great importance has it will help define a better positioning. At point C which is the support level on the 5-minute chart and the VWAP at around $5, but which is quite far from the stop loss. Taking a close look at the 1-minute chart shows that the 9 and 20 EMA around $6.25 could act as a potential support level. If this level get broken, it most likely that price will head lower down toward the VWAP as many day traders will have their stop loss postioned in order to pull them out of the market so as to minimize risk. For the sole purpose of camparism, I have marked out other support level on the 1-minute chart as point C.

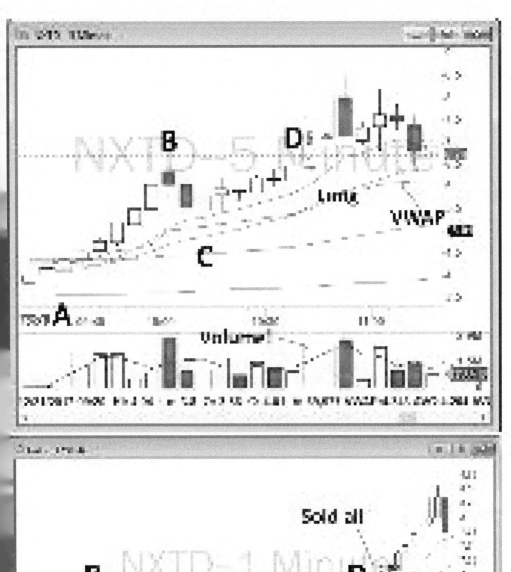

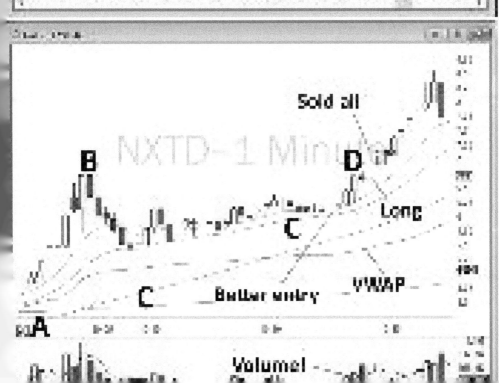

Figure 22 – This shows the ABCD Pattern on NXTD.

This is another illustration of ABCD Patterns which can be seen on Applied Optoelectronics, Inc. (ticker: AAOI) on the 24th of July, 2017, as set forth in Figure 23. I was not able to take this trade, but I have two ABCD Patterns on my 5-minute chart for you to see, which I have marked out on my 1-minute chart. Now, for you to practice, before further reading ahead, I want you to think through the possible trades you could take with these two charts.

Figure 23 - Shows the ABCD and abcd Patterns on AAOI.

After you have studied and practiced this strategy, it will be best if we can do a quick practice run, but now on The Finish Line, Inc. (ticker: FINL) on the 29th of August, 2017, as set out in Figure 24. I did carried out an ABCD Pattern trade on the FINL and I can vividly remember how rewarding the trade was, I made good money from it. I was quite familiar with the trading set ups and carefully identified those set ups on both my 5-minute and 1-minute charts as ABCD, abcd, and áƀćd'.

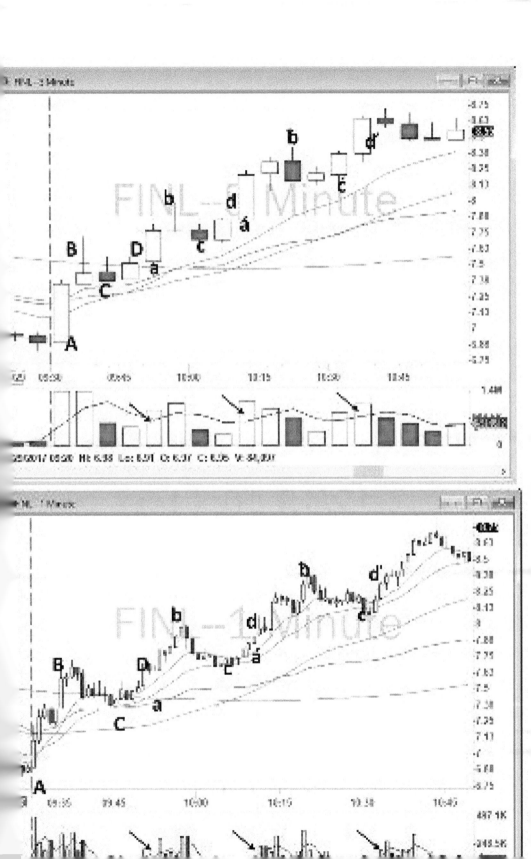

Figure 24 - Shows the ABCD, abcd and áᵬćď Patterns on FINL.
However, I only took the trade on the first pattern; placing the ABCD on the 5-minute chart. The trade was rewarding with a pleasant experience and because of my success I did not need to stay long on the trade. I had my market entry when the price was at $7.50 and exited when price was at $7.98 and $7.80, as shown in Figure 25.

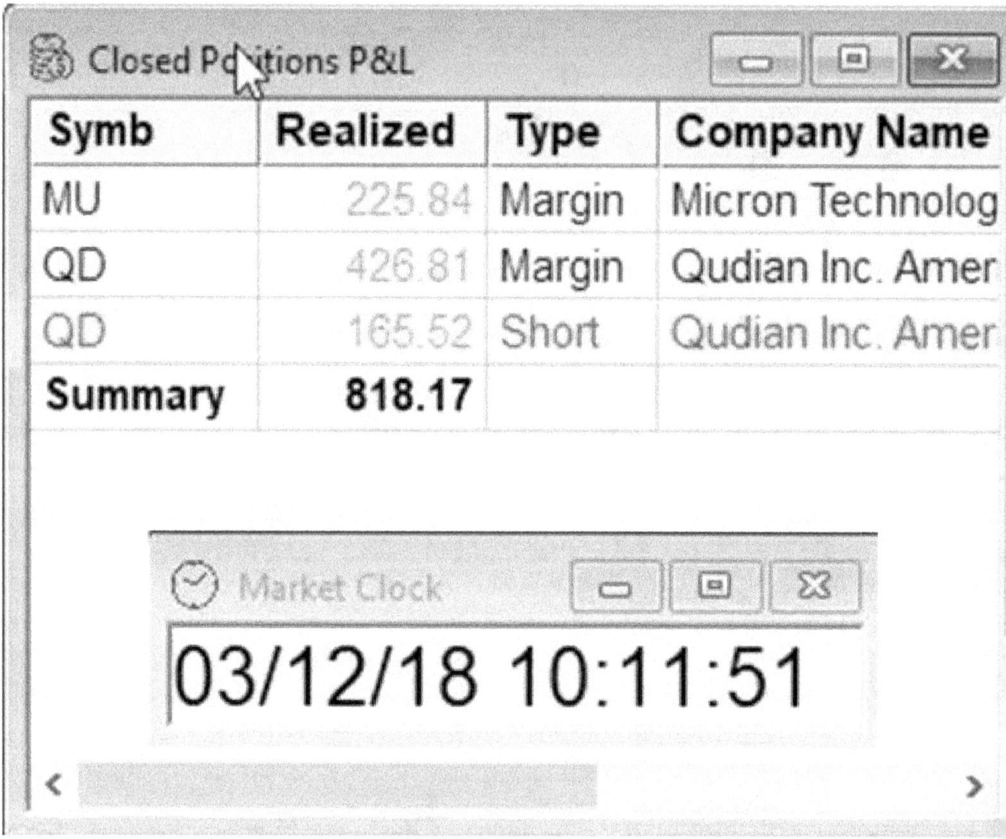

Symb	Realized	Type	Company Name
MU	225.84	Margin	Micron Technolog
QD	426.81	Margin	Qudian Inc. Amer
QD	165.52	Short	Qudian Inc. Amer
Summary	**818.17**		

Closed Positions P&L

Market Clock

03/12/18 10:11:51

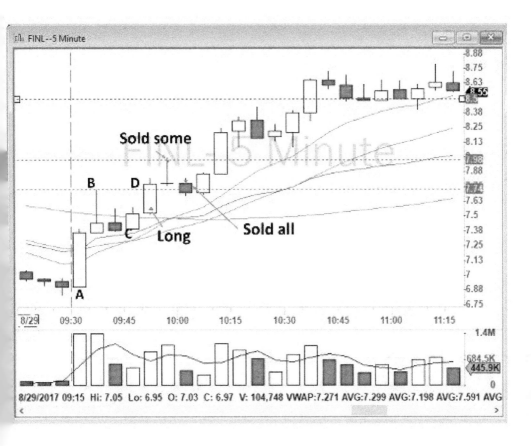

Symb	Realized	Type	Company Name
BBY	84.35	Short	Best Buy Co., Inc. Common S
FINL	1019.01	Margin	The Finish Line, Inc. - Class A
NKE	156.00	Short	Nike, Inc. Common Stock
Summary	**1259.36**		

08/29/17 10:02:03

Figure 26 - My trade on FINL.

Summarizing my trading strategy for ABCD Pattern:

Whenever I find a Stock in Play, which could either from my Gappers watchlist or from any of my scanners, or at times when I'm advised by someone in our chatroom that a stock is most likely be surging up from a certain position (point A) and making a significant uptrend to a new high for the day (point B), I will exercise patience to see if the price could make a support higher than it previous position (at point A). I will refer to this point C. I have always advised against jumping on trades especially when there is a trend. I take my time to watch the stock during its consolidation period. I meticulously chose my share size, the stop loss and profit target exit strategy, as all this will affect the profitabilty of my trade and ensure I stay deciplined throughout my stay in the market. Whenever I realise that price is holding a support at point C, I often enter the trade very close to the price of point C in anticipation of it making an uptrend forward toward point D or even higher. Point C can be easily be identified from a 1-minute chart. It is advisable and encouraged to always look at both time frames in order to gain a better insight of the market action. 4 The stop loss is positioned at the loss of point C. In any situation when the price falls below point C, I will opt to sell and accept the loss that comes therafter. Therefore, it is very important to always strive to buy the stock close to point C in order to minimize the loss incurred. However, some risk averser will wait and confirm before buying only at point D to ensure that the ABCD Pattern is really working. In my opinion, I will not really encourage this conservative approach because it basically reduces your reward while at the same time increases risk.

5 In a situation where the price experiences an upsurge and moves higher, I will opt to selling half of my position at point D, and as a result move my stop loss higher to my entry point to create a break-even.

6 As soon as I reliase that my target profit is hit, I will sell off my remaining position or in the case when I notice the price is losing steam or that the sellers are acquiring more control of the price action. But in the case, when I see that the price makes a new low on my 5-minute chart, with this it can only be that buyers are almost exhausted which is such a relief and a good indicator.

Reverse ABCD Pattern;

The Reverse ABCD Pattern is a mirror of the ABCD Pattern but for selling short instead of going long. Thus, all the previously discussed principles, rules and tactics apply equally to both patterns. To demonstrate how a Reverse ABCD Pattern works, let's review Figure 27, which was a trade I took on Amicus Therapeutics, Inc. (ticker: FOLD) on the 4th of October, 2017. At the Open of trade, the stock had a heavy sold off from at a price of $16.50 (at point A) and then experienced the low of the day when the price was at $15.63 (at point B). FOLD later had a consolidation between the low of the day when the price was at $16.08, a level that I had previously identified in the pre-market. As soon as FOLD started toward the previous low of the day when price was at $15.63 (point B), and to make a recent low of the day (point D), I went short and covered my position toward the 200 SMA on my 5-minute chart for an amazing $595 profit. The stop loss in this case was a new 5-minute high or break when the price was at $16.08 (which acted as the resistance level).

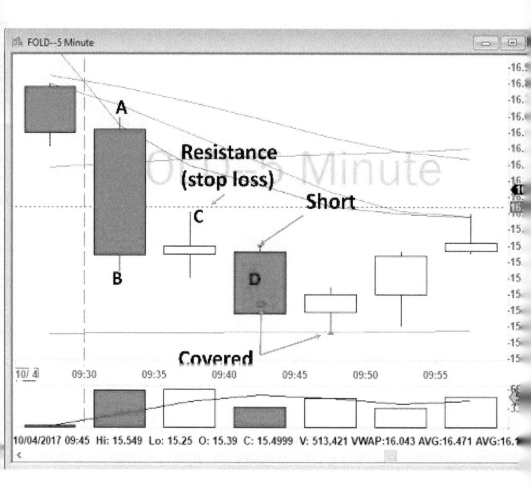

Strategy 3: Bull Flag / Bear Flag

The Bull Flag Strategy is essentially an ABCD Pattern, but the term is often used by some traders who are mostly on low float stocks under $10 (Chapter 3). To ensure I emphasize on the differences, I made it a different strategy in this book. Most of this tactics are essentially the same as for the ABCD Pattern. The duration of trade seems like the only real differences between this strategies. The risk level of the bull Flags are often difficult to manage, just beacuse they happen much faster and the trades are very volatile. As a result it thus requires a very fast execution platform and a fast decision-making process. I have always tried to discourage new traders to from trading low float stocks at the beginning of their trading career.

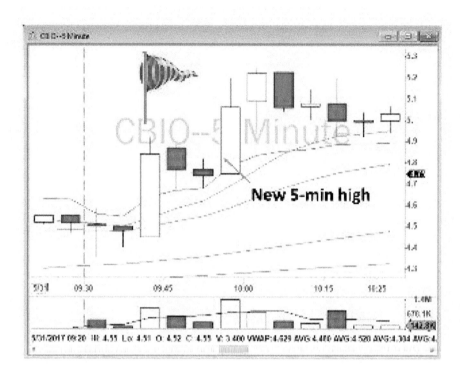

New 5-min high

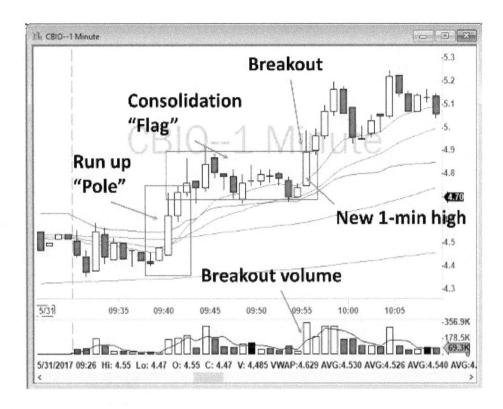

Figure 31 – Shows an Example of a Bull Flag formation with a consolidation period on CBIO.

The Bull Flag appear both on the 1-minute and 5-minute charts. This pattern, appearing in Figure 31 above, can be referred to as the named Bull Flag because it likened to resemble a flag on a pole. In Bull Flag, one or several engulfing candlesticks can be seen to be going up (like a pole), and several smaller candles moving sideways (like a flag), or, as it is genearlly referred to by we day traders as, "consolidating". Consolidation often refer to a market activity whereby traders who bought stocks at a lower price are now selling it for a price greater than what they bought and reaping it profits. Whenever this is happening, the price of the stocks do not decrease sharply because buyers are still in the trade and the sellers do not yet have the full control of the price. Traders who were not opportuned enough to have entered the market before the Bull Flag started will have to wait for another opportunity to be a part of the trade. As a trader, the moment you notice the price starts breaking up in the consolidation area with heavy volume, that is the window for you to go long. Patience truly is a virtue which must be learned in order to become a very successful trader. But how do you find a Bull Flag? Our community use a simple yet effective scanner in Trade Ideas that shows us low float stocks that make a recent high of the day.

93

Usually, the running up phase (pole phase) is the time that it will take a stock to make a new recent high of the day. It is quite possible to find the bull flag before the consolidation period by mere scanning for stocks that make a recent high of the day with relatively heavy volume. Jumping on trades and trend should be avoided as I have alway emphasized, even when your scanner get hit by a low float stock. Buying a stock when the price is "running up" is so risky and trader should always avoid this, as it is not wise enough. This is referred to as chasing the stock. Looking for a quiet time to make entry is basically on of the key strategy of professional traders, in order to take their profits during the volatile times. This act is one of the key defining strategies that differentiates an amateur from a professional, as this is the total opposite of how amateurs trade. Amatuer traders are always fond of jumping in and out of trades and trends whenever the stocks begin to run, become bored and lose interest when the prices of stocks are, shall I say, sleepy. Chasing the stocks is an account killer for beginners.

Time	Symbol	Price ($)	Vol Today	Rel Vol	Flt (Shr)
M History: High of the Day Bull Flag					
9:52:49 AM 3/13/2018	UUM	1.42	141.325	5.06	53.4M
9:50:19 AM 3/13/2018	PTI	6.88	8.09M	90.86	21.1M
9:48:24 AM 3/13/2018	PTI	6.79	7.48M	88.75	21.1M
9:47:43 AM 3/13/2018	SSC	2.01	1.00M	11.30	29.4M
9:47:16 AM 3/13/2018	VNET	8.75	256,792	10.19	83.1M
9:45:26 AM 3/13/2018	PTI	6.68	6.35M	82.48	21.1M
9:44:13 AM 3/13/2018	PTI	6.62	5.89M	81.78	21.1M
9:43:12 AM 3/13/2018	PTI	6.42	5.25M	78.50	21.1M
9:42:34 AM 3/13/2018	FTFT	3.49	110,398	2.14	4.01M
9:42:05 AM 3/13/2018	SSC	1.97	726.042	12.25	29.4M

Figure 32 – Shows an example of my recent High on the Day Scanner.

To serve as a better illustration, let us review the scanner alert on the 13th of March, 2018 for Proteostasis Therapeutics, Inc. (ticker: PTI). As shown in Figure 33, I got the first hit on my scanner at 9:43:12 a.m. Whenever something like this happens, it is best to always check your charts and wait for an excellent

94

opportunity. The mere fact that you got an alert hit on your scanner is no guarantee that the stock is suitable for trading at that moment. Over my years of experience, I have come to reliaze that about 95% scanner alerts are generally not suitable for trade; only about 5% usually provide an excellent risk/reward opportunity. Experienced and professional will exercise caution until they can find a solid consolidation. The goal is always to have a point of entry when there is a breakout with volume. In this instance, it took me about 12 minutes before the true breakout happened at 9:55:10 a.m. The PTI moved when the price of the stock was at $6.90 to over when the price hits $7.20 with heavy volume, as shown in Figure 6.22. The volume of shares traded thereafter was significantly higher after it consolidation, which is a confirmation for a long entry.

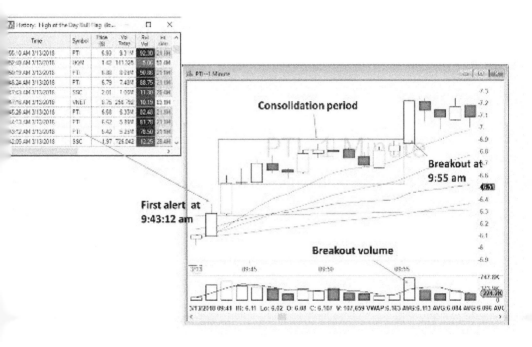

Figure 33 — Shows an example of Scanner alert on PTI and accompanying 1-minute chart.

Usually a Bull Flag should will always show several consolidation periods. I only utilize the first and second consolidation periods as my point of entry into trades. Often in most trades the third and higher consolidation periods are always risky because the stock price must have probably been very extended in a way that indicates that the buyers will soon be losing their control on the market. Let's study an example in Figure 34 below for further clarifications, a Bull Flag on RIGL on the 30th of August, 2016.

95

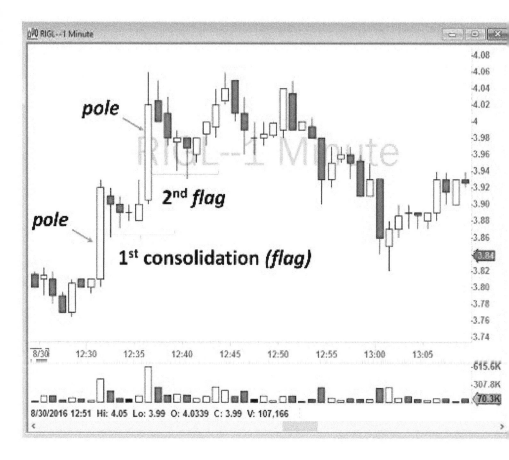

Figure 34 – Shows an example of Bull Flag formation with two consolidation periods on the RIGL.

This shows an example of two Bull Flag Patterns. It is normally quite difficult to catch the first Bull Flag, and you might probably miss it, but as I have previously explained above, you should have your scanner alert you in order to get ready to catch the next Bull Flag. My scanner show the RIGL at 12:36:15 p.m and as soon as I saw that, I realized that there was also a very high relative volume of trade (120 times the normal trading volume), which made this a perfect setup for day trading. I patiently await the end of the first consolidation period and, as soon as I realize the stock started to move toward its high for the day, I saw this as the best point of entry into the trade and I jumped in. My stop loss was the breakdown of the consolidation period. I marked out my point of entry and exit in Figure 35 below.

96

Figure 35 – Shows the entry point, the stop loss and exit for a Bull Flag Strategy on RIGL.

This shows another eaxmple of the Bull Flag which can be seen on NVFY on the 6th of April, 2017, as set out in Figure 36. You will notice that NVFY made an uptrend and ran up at the Open making a strong move when the price was at $1.85 to over $2.30. It showed a consolidation that held for about 20 minutes and then eventually broke the consolidation with a new 5-minute high and heavy volume with a price of $2.60.

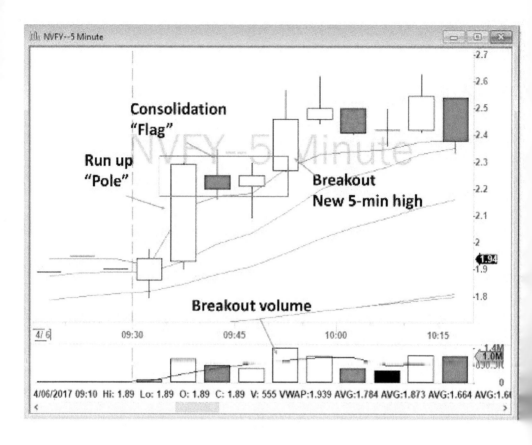

Figure 36 – Shows an example of a Bull Flag on NVFY.

This is an additional example of the Bull Flag which can be seen on AEZS on the 19th of July, 2017, as set out in Figure 37. You will notice that AEZS made an uptrend movement shortly after the Open and then showed a consolidation which lasted for an hour before eventually breaking the consolidation with a new 5-minute high and heavy volume. Meanwhile, just after 12 noon, a second Bull Flag occurred which then broke free to make yet another new 5-minute high and again with heavy volume.

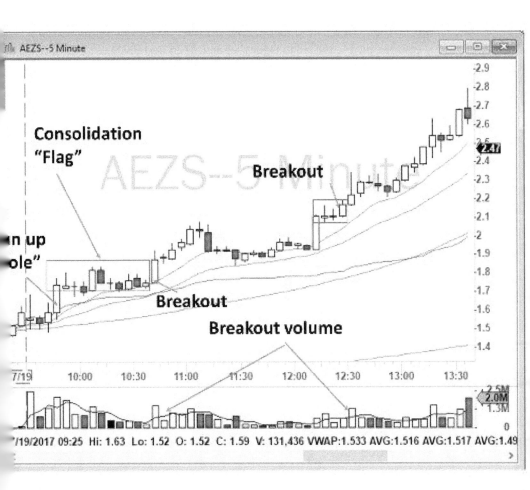

Figure 37 – Shows an Example of a Bull Flag on AEZS.

To become a successful trader this strategy, a perfect point of market entry is essential. Without a perfect entry into the market, this is most likely going to create a bad risk/reward ratio, and will potentially often leads to severe loss of capital. To have a perfect entry into the market when executing the Bull Flag Strategy, it is important for you to have successfully recognize the consolidation period on both your 1-minute and 5-minute charts. If you are not certain that the stocks are consolidating, having an uptrend or experiencing a downtrend, then it is advisable for you not to trade the stock at that moment. This could sometimes mean that the stock is too choppy to trade at that moment.

However, After you have successfully recognize the consolidation period, you need to look for the new 1-minute and 5-minute highs with increasing volume. Sometimes either of the 1-minute or 5-minute chart could show a potential good

99

entry, but it is often best when both of these charts emphasizes and are together in such a way so that a new 1-minute candle coincides with a new 5-minute high with heavy volume, as it is shown in Figure 41 are. AEZS and HMNY.

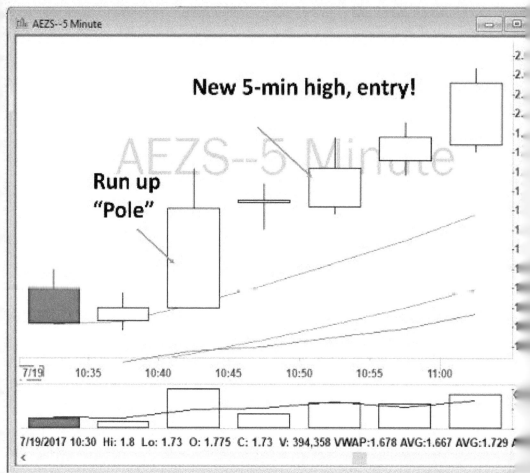

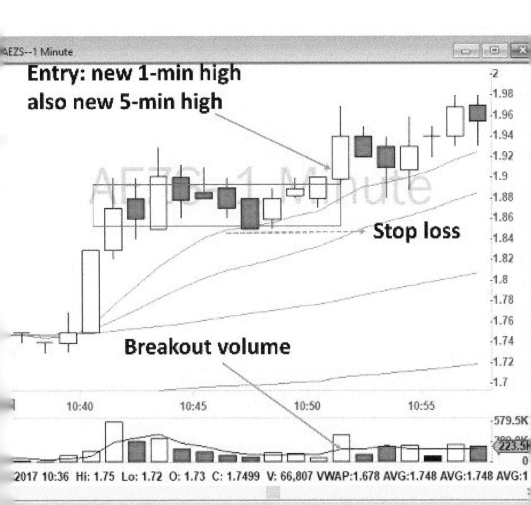

Entry: new 1-min high also new 5-min high

Stop loss

Breakout volume

AEZS--1 Minute

10:40 10:45 10:50 10:55

2017 10:36 Hi: 1.75 Lo: 1.72 O: 1.73 C: 1.7499 V: 66,807 VWAP:1.678 AVG:1.748 AVG:1.748 AVG:1

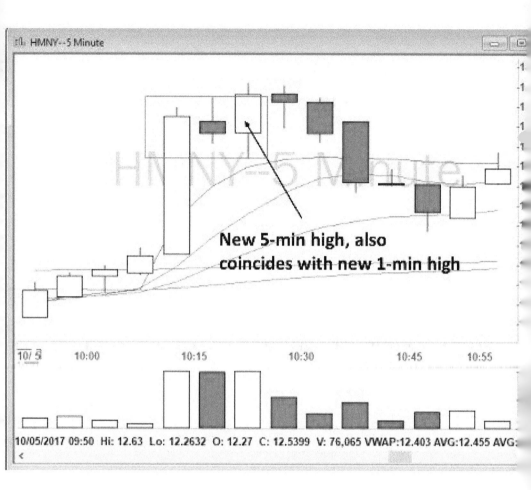

New 5-min high, also coincides with new 1-min high

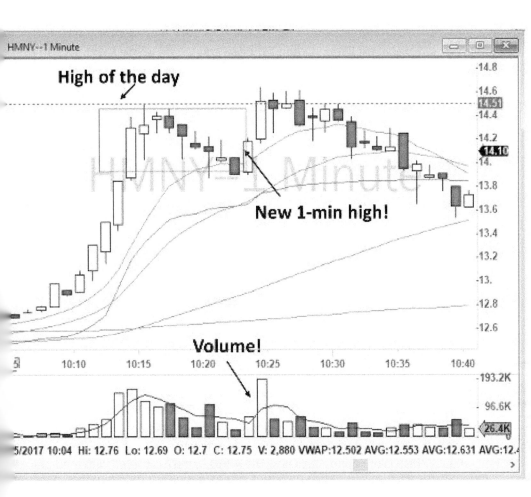

Figure 41 – Shows the Entry points for AEZS and HMNY, where both the 5-minute and 1-minute charts make a recent high (when compared to previous candles) with strong volume. the 1-minute highs are usually less difficult to distinguish. Summarizing this trading strategy:

1. Whenever I see a stock surging up (which could either be on my real time New High of the Day Scanner or when I get advised by someone in our chatroom), I often take my time until I can identify a clean consolidation period. Over the years, I have learned not to jump on trend or into the trade right away (you should have this at the back of your mind that is a dangerous act to "chase stock") because this act will hinder you to put a proper stop loss if you are chasing stock.

2. patiently watch the stock during the consolidation period while I continue to choose my share size, my stop loss and exit strategy.

3. The moment when I realise the prices are moving over the high of the consolidation candles, I see this as my perfect entry to the trade. My stop loss is always placed below the consolidation periods. The perfect entry into the market is usually when both the 1-minute and the 5-minute charts make a recent high at the same time (when it is compared to previous candles). As such It is important to always look at both charts at the same time before executing the trade with this strategy.

4. I sell off 50% of my position with the sole aim to take profit on the way up, usually with a break of the high of the day. After disposing half of my trading position and to prevent any loss, I move my stop loss from the consolidation period to my entry price to create a break-even.

5. After achieveing my target profit or the moment I sense that the stock price is losing steam and that sellers are starting to gain control of the price action, I sell off my remaining positions.

6. In situation where you dont have a target profit, making reference to the 1-minute or 5-minute chart will guide your actions. Look out for when the price makes a new 1-minute or 5-minute low and sell off your positions afterwards.

This is ideal especially when the price roll over and causes a change in the trend. If you take a close look, the Bull Flag is an essential ABCD Pattern that will happen often on low float stocks. However, in a Bull Flag Strategy for stocks whose price is less than $10, many traders will only buy when the price is at or near the breakout (which is the opposite to how the ABCD Pattern is traded with medium float stocks). The obvious reason for this is that moves that occur in low float stocks happen very fast and they often fade away easily. As a result, the Bull Flag is more or less a Scalping Strategy. Scalpers will only buy when a stock is running. They find it difficult to buy during the period of consolidation (which is the waiting and holding phase). For these kind of stocks it is important to only make an entry just when there is a confirmation of a breakout as this stocks often drop brutally and quickly. One of the ways to reduce risk and the time of exposure in low float is to be patient enough for the stock to break the top of the consolidation area. Rather than just buying, witholding and waiting, scalpers will only wait for the perfect window for a breakout and send in their order which will reduce the time of exposure. They only get in when coast is clear, scalp, and get out of the market quickly. That's the fundamental philosophy of momentum scalpers. The Bull Flag Pattern is a long-based strategy that lays within an uptrend in a stock. A similar approach, which is the Bear Flag, can also be defined, but in reverse for short selling. I personally don't take the Bear Flag trade, because most of my brokers do not have low float stock shares available for shoper selling. In addition, you should also note that short selling low float stocks are often accompanied with high level of risk because they have the potential to squeeze significantly to the upside. As such, because of the level of risk and difficulties associated with trading low float stocks, new trader should always be wary whenever they are taking such trade. However, if you see the need for you to make this trade, as I have earlier cautioned, trade only with a very small percentage of your capital and only after sufficient practice in your simulator. These stocks are fast moving stocks as a result you will be required to have a super-fast execution system before taking such trade. Paradoxically, some new traders unfortunately kick off their trading with low float stocks, without proper understanding of the market and most of them are forced to end their career even before it began. I will therefore recommend that new traders, at the start of their trading stay away from this low float stocks, continue to build their account and confidence with trading medium float stocks, and then slowly move toward trading low float stocks in small sizes. It really does not end well well for beginners when they get caught up on the wrong side while trading these low float stocks

Strategy 4: Opening Range Breakout

This is a well-known trading strategy and it is referred to as is the Opening Range Breakout (ORB). This strategy signals the point of entry, but does not really determine the target profit. I will advise that you should define your best profit target based on other technical levels you learn in this book. As we proceed, you will get to notice that I have listed further possibly profit targets. The ORB will only serve just as an entry signal, but always remember that, a full trading strategy must define the proper point of entry, the exit and stop loss. Right at the Open of trade (at 9:30 a.m. New York time), Stocks in Play usually experience violent price action that come as a result of heavy buy and sell orders coming into the market. However, this is usally as a result of heavy trading that comes from traders as well as investors taking profits or loss of the overnight postion in the first five minutes. Some overnight trader will result into selling off their postion for profit the moment they reliase stocks have gapped up. At the same time, some investors might decide to jump into the market to buy the stock before the price goes higher. Also in a situation whereby the stock gaps down, this might cause some investors to panic and dump their shares right at the Open before it drops any lower. However, some institutions might decide to take to the market and acquire share on a large scale thinking the drop could be a good buying opportunity and they will buy large positions at a discounted price. It is therefore a very complicated mass psychology unfolding at the Open for the Stocks in Play. Wise traders will exercise patience and watchout for the opening ranges to develop while they allow other traders to fight each other until one side wins. Typically, it is advised to that you give the opening range at least five minutes. This waiting period is referred to as the 5-minute ORB. Even at this, some traders often like to take their time in order for them to see clearer where the market is heading toward, this might take up to 30 minutes of wait or even longer than that, so as to identify the balance of power between the sellers and the the buyers. They will then develop a trading plan in the direction of the 30-minute or 60-minute breakout. Over my trading years, I am fond of taking trades only at the 5-minute ORB, but lately I am leaning toward the 15-minute ORB and sometimes the 30-minute ORB. You should note that the longer the time frame of the trade, the less volatility you should expect. With most setups, the ORB Strategy has been proven to work best with mid to large cap stocks, which do not often show a wild price swings intraday. Personally, I will strongly recommend against trading this strategy with low float stocks that have the tendency to gapped up or down. Ideally, stock should trade within a range which is usually smaller than the Average True Range of the stock (ATR). The upper and lower boundaries of the range can be identified by the high and low of the 5-, 15-, 30- or 60- minute candles. To have a more comprehensive understanding of this strategy, let's look at Figures 42 and 43 for e.l.f. Beauty, Inc. (ticker: ELF) on the 9th of March, 2017. ELF was on my Gappers watchlist that day, and had gapped up over 19% for good results. In order to see if I could have this trade on the short side, I decided to give it a close watch. There was a very high probability that some overnight traders and investors would attempt to sell their positions. A profit margin of 19% is a very tempting for offer for many overnight investors. So why not take it?

$	T	C $	C %	Float			Sector
30.30	186.010	5.00	19.8	3.556.310	0.90	7.49	Retail Trade
14.00	59.961	-3.02	-17.7	18.08M	0.58	6.54	Manufacturing
16.70	437.617	-6.67	-28.5	48.34M	0.91		Retail Trade

Figure 42 - My Gappers watchlist on the 9th of March, 2017 at 9 a.m. which shows that the ELF may be a Stock in Play for the day.

From figure 43 below, you will see, the stock opened when it price was at $31 and sold off heavily below the price of $30 in the first five minutes. This is a signal that investors have already started selling off thier positions for profit after it had gapped up 19%. I waited and watched the first 5-minute battle unfold between the sellers and the buyers. The moment I notice that the price broke the 5-minute opening range, I went short below the VWAP. And as I have previously mentioned, the ORB is just a buy or sell signal, and you as a trader will have to define your proper exit and the position of your stop loss for it. For me, the position of my stop loss is always a close above the VWAP for short positions, and a break below VWAP for long positions. The position of the profit target is the next important technical level.

from Figure 6.29 below you will see that, I followed the wave down to the next daily level at price of $28.62 and covered my shorts around that level.

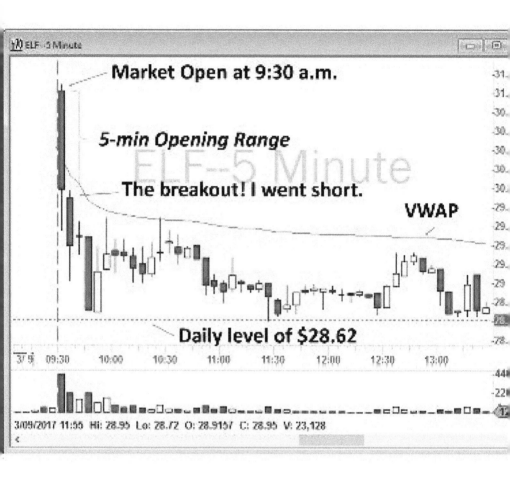

Figure 43 – Shows an Example of the ORB Strategy on the ELF 5-minute chart. Another illustration is the Procter & Gamble Co. (ticker: PG) on the 15th of February, 2017. This stock hit my Scanner, as shown in Figure 44, and I had it on my watchlist at the Open.

bol	S	T..l	C $	C %	Flow	ll.'l I	SFlow	Sector
A	50.70	107,445	3.35	7.1	20.93M	1.04	5.78	Manufacturing
	89.44	449,389	1.58	1.8	2.56B	0.79	1.37	Manufacturing
	63.10	552,600	-3.79	-5.7	1.03B	0.81	1.45	Finance and Insurance
	18.71	702,161	-4.16	-18.2	33.89M	1.11	35.88	Wholesale Trade

Figure 44 – Shows my Gappers watchlist on the 15th of February, 2017 at 9 a.m. This shows that PG may be a Stock in Play for the day. From Figure 45, you can see that, just in the first five minutes of trade more than 2.6 million shares were traded, but the stock price only moved from $89.89 to $89.94, a range of just 5 cents, while the Average True Range (ATR) of PG was at $0.79. As I have earlier mentioned, you need to have the opening range smaller than the daily ATR. When stocks move closer or higher than its ATR at the Open, it is not a good strategy for the ORB. This could only mean that the stock is too volatile and without a catchable move. It is worth of mentioning that Stocks in Play move, and these moves are directional and catchable. When a certain stock is constantly changing directions, moving up and down at price of $2 with high volume, but without any directional signal, it advisable for you to stay away from such stock. Stocks like these are usually heavily traded by computers. In the example of the PG stocks, the moment I reliase that it broke the opening range to the upside, I went long and followed up with the wave towards the resistance level at the price of $91.01. Sometimes during trades, it is advised that you exit when a stock shows some signs of weakness and there is no obvious technical level for the exit and target profit. For example, you should consider selling if you are long and price makes a new 5-minute low, this could only mean that the stock is showing some weakness. However, some market action could only signal strenght and the perfect time to cover your postion, especially when you are going short and the stock makes a new 5-minute high. With this PG illustration of the market, if you were unable to previously identify the $91.01 level, you could exit the trade when it made the new 5-minute low just below $91. I marked this out for you in Figure 45 below.

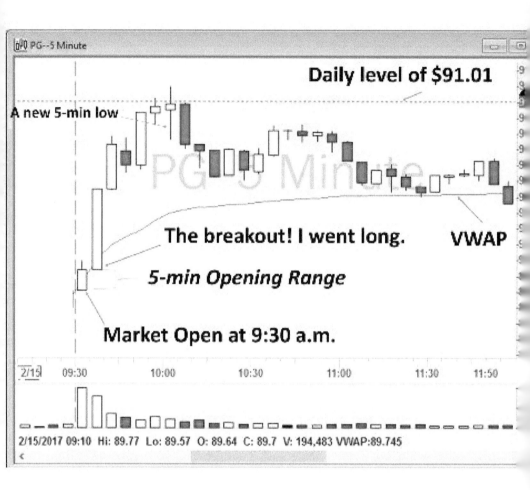

Figure 45 – Shows an Example of the ORB Strategy on the PG 5-minute chart.

Summarizing my ORB Strategy:

1. After building my watchlist in the morning, I do closely monitor my shortlisted stocks for the first five minutes after the Open. I pay a close attention to them and identify their opening range with their respective price action. What is the number of shares being traded? Is it jumping up and down or is the stock experiencing a directional upward or downward movement? Is the stock of high volume with large orders only, or are there numerous orders going through? I have always prefered to trade stocks that have high volume, but also with numerous orders being traded. As a retail trader, you should watch out for the numbers of orders tthat have been trade with the stock and not just the volume alone. A stock could have traded 1 million shares, but those shares could have been only ten orders of 100,000 shares, this is not a liquid stock to trade. The Volume of share alone do not define it liquidity; the number of orders that are being sent to the exchange is also an important factor. The opening range must

be smaller than the stock's Average True Range (ATR). I placed ATR as a column in my Trade scanner. After the first five minutes of trading has closed, the stock may still continue to be traded in that opening range for the next five minutes. But, at times when I notice that the stock is breaking the opening range, I will enter the trade according to the direction of such breakout: long for an upward breakout and short for a downward move.

4) My stop loss is always positioned from a close below the VWAP for the long positions and a just break above VWAP for the short positions.

5) My targeted profit is the next important technical level, which includes as: (1) An important intraday daily levels that I identify in the pre-market, (2) Moving averages on a daily chart, and/or (3) Previous day close.

6) Without a defined technical level for an exit and the profit target, I will exit the trade when the stock starts to shows some signs of weakness (if I go long) or strength (when I go short). For instance, when the price makes a new 5-minute low, that is a sign of weakness shown by the stock,this will make me consider selling my position if I was going long. If I was short and the stock makes a new 5-minute high, this could only signal strength and I consider covering my position. This same strategy will be applicable for the 15-minute or 30-minute ORBs.

Strategy 5: VWAP Trading

What is VWAP? Volume Weighted Average Price, or VWAP, is one of the most important and reliable technical indicator for day traders. VWAP is a mathematical indicator that is calculated by adding up the dollars traded for every transaction (which is the price multiplied by number of shares traded) and dividing the total shares traded for the day. I will be skipping explaining VWAP in real mathematical terms, but essentially, VWAP is a moving average that takes into account the total volume of the shares being traded at any price for the day. Other moving averages are usually calculated based on the price of the stock traded on the chart, but VWAP takes into consideration the number of shares in the stock per price that are being traded. As a day trader you should ensure that your trading platform have the VWAP built into it and without alerting any of its default settings. VWAP is a tool that helps to indicate who is in control of the price action – which is either the buyers or the sellers. When there is a high buying demand on a stock, it mean that the buyers are in overall control of the price and such stock is usually traded above the VWAP. However when the price of a stock breaks below the VWAP, you can assume that the sellers are starting to gain control over the price action of the stock. VWAP is a trading tool that is employed to measure the performance of institutional traders. Professional and well-expierenced traders who work for investment banks or hedge funds and who are required to trade in large numbers of shares everyday cannot enter or exit the market by just a single order. The level of liquidity of the market is not enough for this trader to enter a one million share by an order. Therefore, this trade will often need to liquidate their orders gradually during the day. This institutional traders will regularly need to compare their prices to VWAP values after they have bought or sold a large position of stocksduring the day. Any order to buy which is executed below the VWAP would be considered as a good fill for them because such stock was bought below an average price (which means that such trader bought the stock in large position at a relatively discounted price when compared to the market). Conversely, any sell order which is executed above the VWAP would also be deemed to be a good fill because the sell was made above the average price. As a result, the VWAP is often used by institutional traders to identify good point of entry and exit. Therefore, Institutional traders with large orders try to make a buy or sell around the VWAP. The price by which this traders fill their large orders at, is a measure used to evaluate their performance. Any trader who was not able to buy below the the VWAP may be penalized because this action will cost the institution money for taking the large position. Therefore, Institutional traders strive to buy below or as close to VWAP as possible. Conversely, when professional traders have to get rid of large position, they strive to sell at the VWAP or as higher as possible. Any day trader who is aware of this move by institutional traders may benefit from this market activity. The stock in play is usually traded heavily during the first five minutes after the market open usually at or around the VWAP. Individual shareholders, investment banks or hedge funds often monitor the market to see when the Stock in Play gaps up in order to sell their position for the highest possible profit before there is a fall in price. At the same time, some other investors who want to take positions in the trade will want to buy the stock as soon as possible, before the price goes higher. As a result, the first five minutes of trade experience an unknown heavy trading activity happening between the overnight shareholders and the new investors. Scalpers usually read this moment and ride on the momentum right at the Open. After the volatility of the market decreases at about ten to fifteen minutes into the Open, the stock will then move toward or away from the VWAP. This is a test time to see if any large investment bank willing to buy large postion or sell off their postion. If there is any large institutional trader who is willing to buy a significant position, then the stock will move over the VWAP or even much higher. When such activity happen, it is one of the best opportunity for us as day traders to go long on the trade. Conversely, if these large shareholders and investors are wanting to get rid of their positions, then this is a good point to liquidate their positions. When they start to sell off their shares at the VWAP. The price will reject the VWAP and it will start to fall.

This action of the large shareholder will make it an excellent short selling opportunity for day traders. The price of such stock may drift sideways near the VWAP when there is no reasonable intersest from market makers or institutions. As a day trader it will be wise for you to stay away from stocks like this. Trading based on the VWAP has become very easy even for beginner because so many professional traders study the VWAP and make efficient and effective trading decisions based on it. Therefore, this will ensure that a beginner trader will easily be on the right side of trade. In a situation, whereby a stock attempt to break the VWAP but could not, you can go short on the stock because it is safe to assume that the other traders that are also watching will also begin to go short.

Any trading strategy based on VWAP becomes simple and easy strategy to follow. I usually go short on trade when stocks but fail to break the VWAP on the 5-minute charts. Let's have a look at Figure 46 which documents a trade that I took on SolarCity Corporation (ticker: SCTY) on The 24th of June, 2016.

Figure 46 – Shows an Example of a long VWAP Strategy on SCTY

At around 10:30 a.m on the 24th of June, 2016, I noticed that SCTY had a support above VWAP when the price was at $21. I bought 1,000 shares of this stock with the anticipation of the price moving toward $22 with VWAP as my support level. My stop loss was a 5-minute candlestick just below VWAP. At first, I sold off 50% of my position when the price was at $21.50, and then moved my stop loss to create a break-even. I also sold off another position at $22 because I know half-dollars (such as $1.50, $2.50, $3.50) and whole dollars ($1, $2, $3) usually act as the support and resistance level. VWAP also works quite well when you want to go short on stocks. So Let's have a look at Figure 47, which documents another

114

trade that I took on SCTY, this time on the 22nd of June, 2016, and this time it was on the short side.

Figure 47 – Shows an Example of a short VWAP Strategy on SCTY

At around 11 a.m., I noticed that SCTY faced a resistance over VWAP. As a result I shorted the stock with the anticipation of losing the VWAP when the price was at $23. By 12 p.m., the buyers gave up the control of the price, only for the sellers to take over. I had an amazing run down to $22 and covered my shorts when price was at $22 for an awesome $1,000 profit. These examples demonstrate how the VWAP is one of the most important and reliable market indicators for day trading. Please note that the VWAP is just an intraday indicator; as such the VWAP has no meaning on daily or weekly charts. As a result of this, I will expect you to ask this question, how do I make of use VWAP for day trading? I only make use of VWAP as an important support and resistance level for my point entry, stop loss levels and for profit target. I make use of this three strategies based on the principle of VWAP which I will explain below: (1) VWAP False Breakouts, (2) VWAP Reversals, and (3) VWAP Moving Average Trend.

VWAP False Breakout

This is my favorite trading strategy and is referred to as VWAP False Breakout. VWAP False Breakouts; this breakout occur usually during the Late-Morning session of the market, just after 10:30 a.m., and goes on to the early part of the afternoon. When there is pressure from Institutional traders, strong stocks in play will stay and trade right above the VWAP as it is shown in Figure 46. If any large investment bank or shareholder is keen on taking position, such stock will as a result saty above the VWAP and keep moving further above as it is shown in Figure 46 on SCTY. But in situations whereby there are no large institutions putting pressure on the stock, or when this investors have filled in all of their orders and decided to stay off the market after the morning trade session, then such stock be forced to move back to the VWAP and "lose it", meaning the price will fall and trade below the VWAP. This is a signal that short sellers should start going short. After the stock had lost some of its big buyers during the morning session and the price of the stock has fallen below the VWAP, such stock can only be likened to a strong but bleeding buffalo that has ran out of breath. Without doubts, wolves will be waiting and watching as such buffalo struggles to catch it breath, getting ready for their final ambush. This can be Similar to day traders who are monitoring such stock and can "smell the blood" as the strong Stock in Play that was previously above the VWAP suddenly loses it price below it. Sellers who are willing to go short will see this as a perfect opportunity to go short on the stock. With the same example, day traders will look for stocks that has lost their price below VWAP to sell short just like the scavenging vultures will do while waiting for the wolves to finish feast on the unfortunate buffalo. However, when a stock that has previously lost it price below the VWAP is coming back up and gaining momentum toward and above the VWAP, short sellers will desperately need to cover. Smart and experience day traders will this as an opportunity to chase the fleeing shorts by going long to ride the momentum and "squeeze the shorts". Reviewing the Figure 48, the trading behavior of AAOI on the 19th of April, 2017. As you can see, the stock opened weak and sold off below the VWAP toward a daily level with price at $43.61. After bouncing back from the resistance level three times, the stock finally traded above VWAP from around 11:45 a.m. to 12:15 p.m. However, this stock (AAOI) wasn't strong enough to stay above the VWAP and in order to establish a moving average in an upward direction above it. It therefore bounced back from the previous day close of $44.20 (as you can recall from Chapter 4, the previous day close can be at a very strong resistance and support level) and then lost VWAP when the price falls and traded below it.

That VWAP False Breakout shows a sign for trader to go short below the VWAP, for example when price was at $43.75, with a stop loss just above VWAP. The first profit target could be set at the new low of the day, and then later the next daily level when price was at $43.21, as marked in Figure 48.

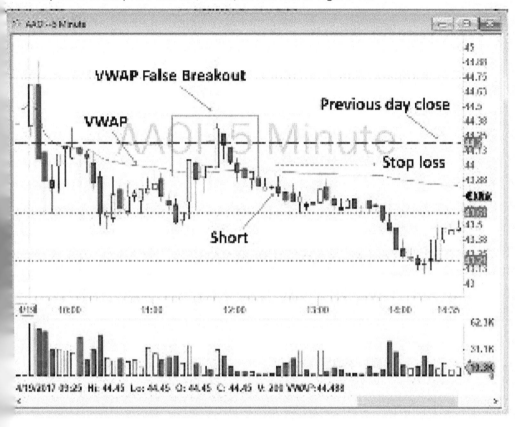

Figure 48 – Shows an Example of VWAP False Breakout on AAOI.

This is Another example which can be seen in Figure 49, a trade showing on the 12th of May, 2017 for the giant American departmental store chain Nordstrom, Inc. (ticker: JWN). As you see, the stock opened weak and sold off below the VWAP toward a daily level when the price was at $41.52 and after the stock bounced back from the resistance level, it bounced above VWAP and traded above it from around 10:05 a.m. to 10:45 a.m. However, JWN was not too strong to have stayed above the VWAP for long in order to establish a moving average with an uptrend movement. So the stock bounced back from a very strong resistance level of 50 Simple Moving Average (50 SMA) and lost the VWAP. This signaled a trading opportunity to go short below the VWAP, for instance when the price was around $42.20, with the stop loss set above the VWAP. The first profit target could be placed when JWN made a new low of the day, and later the next daily level of $41.52, it was marked out as seen in Figure 49.

Figure 49 – Shows an Example of VWAP False Breakout on JWN. Continuing with this discussion of American retail stores, let's review the in Figure 50, which shows the trading of Target Corporation (ticker: TGT) on the 17th of May, 2017. TGT experienced a gap up in the pre-market as a result of good earnings report, but opened weak and sold off below the VWAP when the price was at $55.50, perhaps this could be the after effects of investors and overnight swing traders taking heavy profit. Nevertheless, buyers jumped into the market at around 10 a.m. and TGT stock bounced back strongly after forming an Engulfing Bullish Pattern (Chapter 5) and traded right above the VWAP from around 10:05 a.m. to 10:30 a.m. However, TGT was not strong enough to make a stand and stay above the VWAP to establish a moving average uptrend. As a result it sold off quickly and lost the VWAP. This could only be a sign for sellers to go short below the VWAP, for instance when price was at $56.13, with it stop loss positioned above the VWAP. The first point of target profit could be when TGT make a new low of the day, and later the 200 SMA on the 5-minute chart, as it did sold off by 1:35 p.m., as it was marked out in Figure 50.

Figure 50 – Shows an Example of VWAP False Breakout on TGT.

This is another clear VWAP False Breakout example which is shown in Figure 51 for Adobe Systems Incorporated, American computer software company (ticker: ADBE), on the 21st of June, 2017. ADBE started strong enough to squeezed above the VWAP, but with time, the buyers could not hold onto the trade and lost the battle and the stock closed below the VWAP. As a result, the sellers gained control of the stock price and forced the stock price lower than the VWAP to make the low of the day at $144.23. However, the stock fought back to reverse the action of the sellers and moved toward the VWAP and in fact established trade above it from 10: 00 further to 10:30 a.m. At around 10:30 a.m., the price experienced a bounced back from 20 EMA to go below the VWAP. I was on this trade, took it short below the VWAP with my stop loss positioned above it. The first profit target came at the low of the day when price was at $144.23 and the final target profit was 200 SMA on the 5-minute chart. Unfortunately, I did not exercise enough patience to capture the profit target, but later about 12:25 p.m., it hit the 200 SMA at with the price at $143.50.

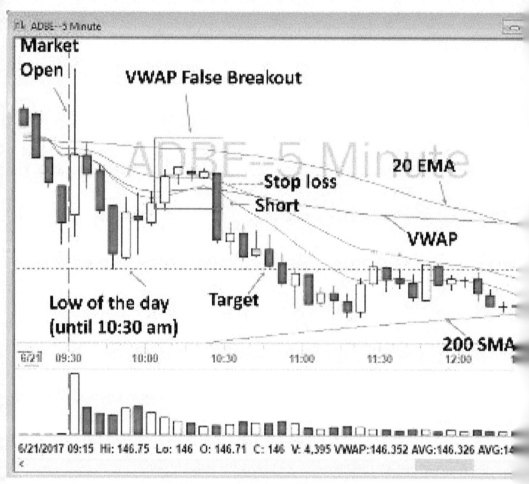

Figure 51 – Shows an example of VWAP False Breakout on ADBE.
This is another perfect illustration shown in the Figure 52 Inc. (ticker: BBBY) on the 23rd of June, 2017. do you think you will be able to identify the VWAP False Breakout?

Figure 52 – Shows an example of VWAP False Breakout on BBBY.

This is another perfect illustration which can be seen in Figure 53, the trade behavior of Alcoa Corporation (ticker: AA) on the 18th of January, 2018 when AA stock squeezed above the VWAP twice; the first just around 10:05 a.m and the second at 10:45 a.m. These two breakouts were unable to break past the 50 SMA on the 5-minute chart and just had to bounced back below the VWAP, providing traders the opportunity to sell short. The first VWAP False Breakout could not reach the previous low of the day with the price at $52.10 (it was also the low of the pre-market). However, the second VWAP False Breakout came and was able to make an excellent short from VWAP to the recent low of the day and went below that.

121

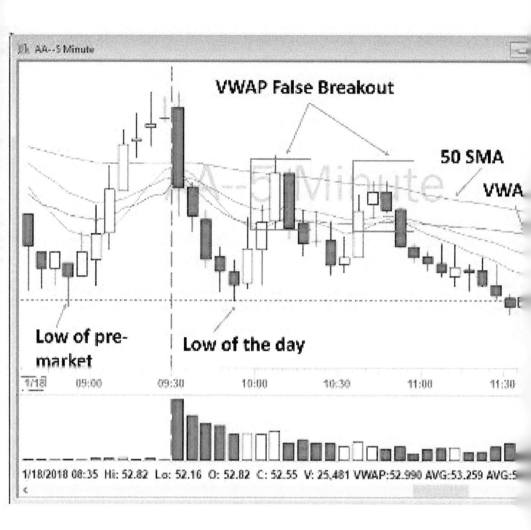

Figure 53 – Shows an Example of VWAP False Breakouts on AA.

Summarizing my trading strategy for the VWAP False Breakouts:

After I have outlined my watchlist for the day, all I did was to monitor the price action around the VWAP at the Open and during the morning session for Stocks in Play. A good Stock in Play often have respect toward the VWAP.

When buyers were in control of the market and force sellers to cover. This could mean that the Stock in Play sold off below the VWAP but was able to bounce back and breaks out above the VWAP. However, if the stock loses the VWAP again in the Late-Morning sesseion(which is from 10:30 a.m. to 12 p.m.), this could mean that at this time that buyers are already weak and exhausted. This provides a short opportunity with the stop loss above VWAP.

The profit target can be positioned at the previous low of the day, or any important technical level.

122

I often ensure I go short when a Stock in Play has loses the VWAP. At some point, I go short even before the price loses the VWAP, to have a good point entry while it is ticking down toward the VWAP in anticipation of a VWAP loss. However, you should always remember that the job of a trader is to identify and not anticipate. Take a small volume of trade and add more share on the way down even after you have truly identified a good trading setup.

VWAP Reversals

Stocks in Play has always be known to trade heavily at the Open and establish an Opening Range Breakout. It is often either they move toward a recent low of the day or stay above the VWAP and go ahead to make a constant high of the day. Either way, they will often reverse and move towards testing the VWAP. This strategy is usally refered to as the VWAP Reversal and can either be traded both on the long side or on the short side of trade. Examining Figure 54, which show the trading behavior of JD.com, Inc. (ticker: JD) on the 13th of November, 2017. JD opened strong, but sold off heavily around 9:35 a.m with an engulfing Bearish Pattern. This stock sold off heavily below the VWAP till 9:50 a.m. when it was 9:50 a.m., it was unable to make a new 5-minute low and this altered the market direction. This seems like the time any Stock in Play will bounce back and challenge the VWAP, making it quite suitable for a VWAP Reversal trade. I was on this trade and decided to go long when the price was at $41.15 and rode the momentum toward the VWAP and higher above it.

But what makes a stock have a reversal toward the VWAP? In a situation like this, many short sellers must have been hoping that the stock price would go lower, but when it doesn't, all of these sellers will have to cover fast, their action will result into causing the stock price to squeeze back up real quick. This is often referred to as "squeezing the shorts". If you had JD short at the Opening Range Breakout, you will want to secure the trade and enusre it does not go against you and definitely want to take the proper profit. This is as a result of staying short while the 5-minute trend becomes altered (which is unable to make the recent 5-minute low, or establishing higher highs and higher lows), then you may get squeezed.

What signals a reversal? When stocks are unable to make the recent 5-minute low, this signals a reversal or, even better, in situations where price begins to make the higher highs and the higher lows on a 5-minute chart, this could only mean that the sellers are getting exhausted and the price will bounce back toward the VWAP. However, just like any other trading strategies, there are some exclusions to this rules where this strategy will not work. In some instances, the price of the stock might not be in your favour and go ahead to make a recent low of the day.

Therefore, it is of utmost importance that when you are trading with this strategy, as well as all strategies, that you ensure you identify a proper stop loss.

Whenever you decide to take trade to the long side, you can define your stop loss just below the low of the day or the previous 5-minute candle low. To identify a proper postion for your profit target, the first target can be placed at the 9 or 20 EMA if there is any and, if not, you should just cover the VWAP. I always ensure that I have some position available for a squeeze above VWAP.

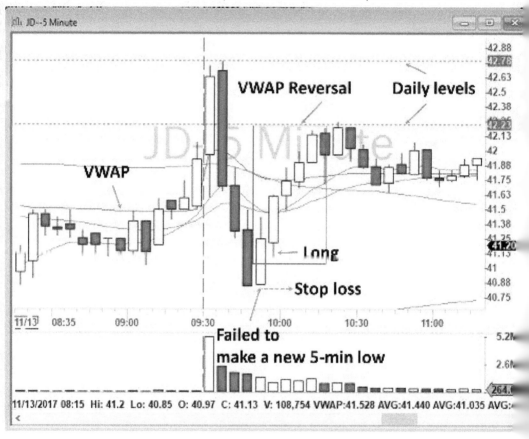

Figure 54 – Shows an Example of VWAP Reversal on JD.

This is an example of a trade I took on Dollar Tree, Inc. (ticker: DLTR) on the 7th of March, 2018. The DLTR sold off heavy volume below the VWAP but experience a standstill when the price was around the resistance level at $88.10 and was unable to make a recent low. I traded long at $88.60, with a profit target of VWAP around $89.70, with a subtantial profit of $409 in a 400 shares, as shown in Figure 55. In this situation, monitoring my 1-minute chart helped me get a better point of entry after DLTR closed above 9 EMA on my 1-minute chart.

124

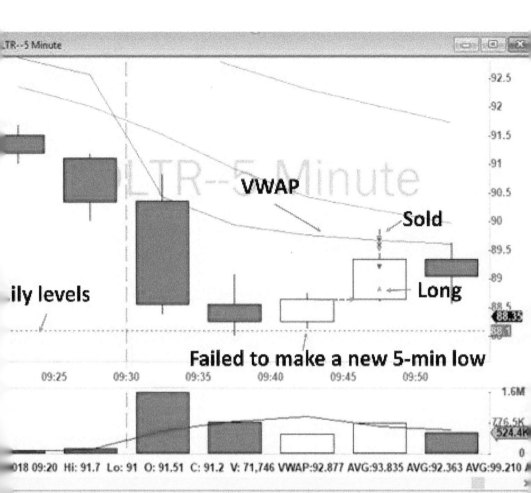

Failed to make a new 5-min low

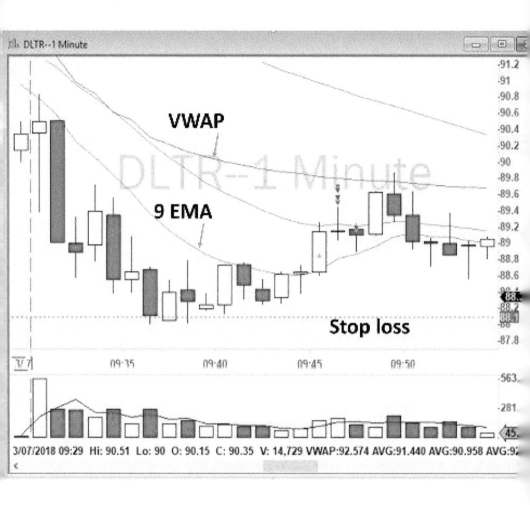

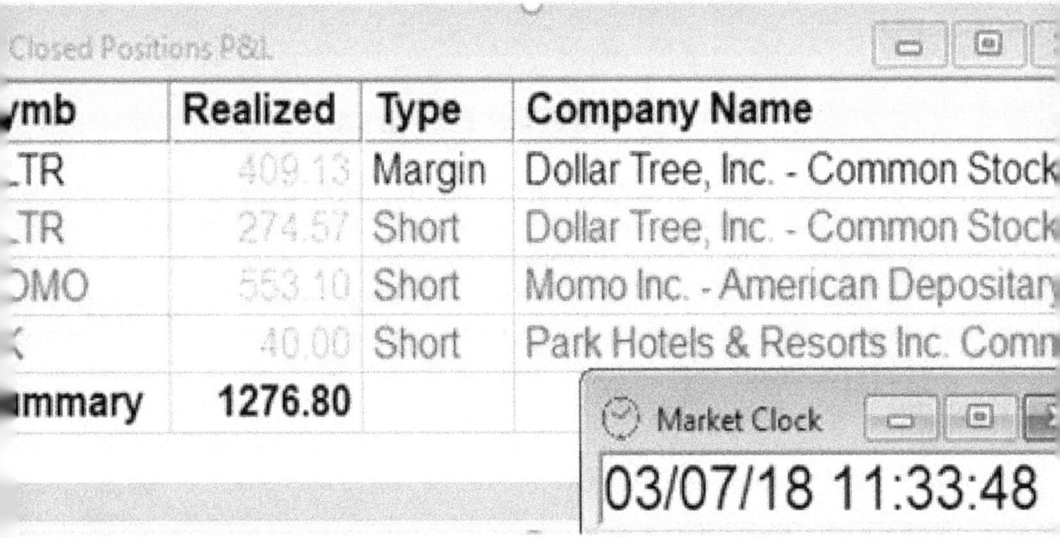

ymb	Realized	Type	Company Name
.TR	409.13	Margin	Dollar Tree, Inc. - Common Stock
.TR	274.57	Short	Dollar Tree, Inc. - Common Stock
)MO	553.10	Short	Momo Inc. - American Depositary
(	40.00	Short	Park Hotels & Resorts Inc. Comn
ımmary	1276.80		

Market Clock

03/07/18 11:33:48

Figure 56 – Shows an Example of the VWAP Reversal on DLTR.

This shows Another example on Alcoa Corporation (ticker: AA) on the 18th of January, 2018. AA had an heavy sold off below the VWAP, but stalled around the resistance level when price was at $52.10, and was unable to make a recent low. Interestingly, $52.10 was also the low on pre-market trade. AA was unable to make a new low, but the stock experienced a trend on my 5-minute chart, reversed and became bullish, making higher highs and higher lows. A good point of entry would be found by monitoring the 1-minute chart when the stock closed above the 9 EMA on the 1-minute chart, with a stop loss placed just below the low of the day and the profit target at the VWAP when the price hits $52.80. A risk/reward ratio of 2 should be expected, as it shown in Figure 56.

Achieving an excellent market entry as well as a favorable risk/reward is extremely a key factor in this strategy. However,some Stock in Play are fond of having a reverse back to the VWAP, but these moves usually are not catchable, these moves happen so quick and are very strong that you cannot be so sure of a perfect market entry with a proper risk/reward. As a trader, you should have it at the back of your mind that you cannot catch all moves nor should you try to be in all of them. Some stocks in play will make good reversal but would not have a great entry point, such trades are better left. In the chatroom, I do see that some trends and moves are correct but still, I wont take them. Sometimes People get baffled by this, but my response is always the same.

Even when I am positive about the direction where the stock will move, but if I cannot spot a perfect entry point, I will let the trade slide. I also think you should do the same.

127

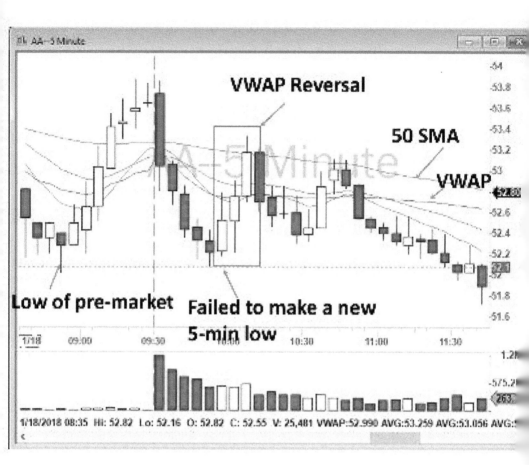

VWAP Reversal

50 SMA

VWAP

Low of pre-market **Failed to make a new 5-min low**

1/18/2018 08:35 HI: 52.82 Lo: 52.16 O: 52.82 C: 52.55 V: 25,481 VWAP:52.990 AVG:53.259 AVG:53.056 AVG:

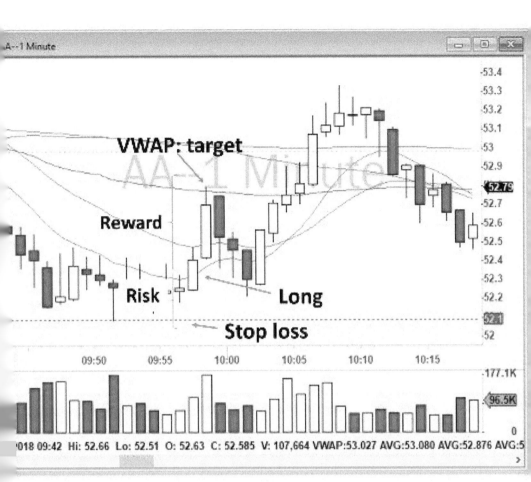

Figure 58 and 59 – Shows the AA VWAP Reversal on both the 5-minute and the 1-minute charts with it risk/reward analysis on the 1-minute chart.

Another illustration is shown on Energous Corporation (ticker: WATT) on the 2nd of January, 2018, as seen in Figure 57. WATT expirenecd an heavy sold off below the VWAP at 9:30 a.m but had a standstill and was unable to make the recent 5-minute low between 9:35 a.m and 9:40 a.m. Monitoring my 1-minute chart, I spotted a good long entry with price at $21 which was possible when the new 1-minute high made a move toward the VWAP at when price hit $22. WATT was able to squeezed hard above the VWAP with price at $23.60. It is best to take profit at the VWAP and let certain percentage of the position run above the VWAP as well. When there is any noticeable level above the VWAP, which includes the moving average of daily levels, it is quite safe to believe that certain stock will challenge those levels.

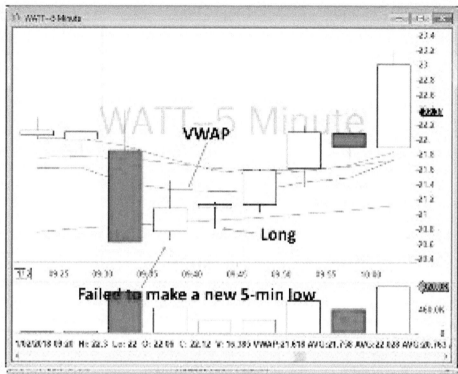

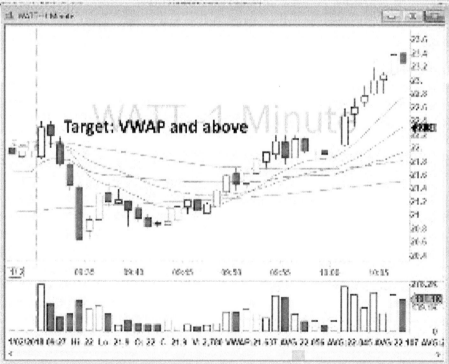

Figure 60 – Shows an Example of VWAP Reversal on the WATT.

I dicretely selected this examples for stocks that had reversal below the VWAP. A pattern likened to this often happen when the stock goes above the VWAP at the Open but was unable to make the recent high of the day or a new 5-minute high. This provides sellers an opportunity to go short on trade towards the VWAP as it is shown in Figure 61 for financial services and mobile payment company Square, Inc. (ticker: SQ). You could see in Figure 61, SQ experiened a decent run at the Open when price was at $36.90 but also was unable to a recent high. This create an opportunity for sellers to go short toward VWAP.

Figure 61 – Shows an Example of VWAP Reversal on SQ.

This is an another great illustration showing the trading behavior of Signet Jewelers Limited, one of the world's largest retailer of diamond jewelry (ticker: SIG), as set in Figure 62. The stock experienced a very impressive strong move at the Open when the stock price was at $57.80 but was unable to hold those highs and begins to make lower lows on the 5-minute chart. This market action show signs of a decent opportunity to sell short. As a result of this market actions, I decided that it would be best if I go short at $57.10 with my stop loss just above the high of the day with my target profit of below the VWAP. Toward the day high, SIG sold off heavily. My first target profit was positioned in such a way that it would cover my short at the VWAP.

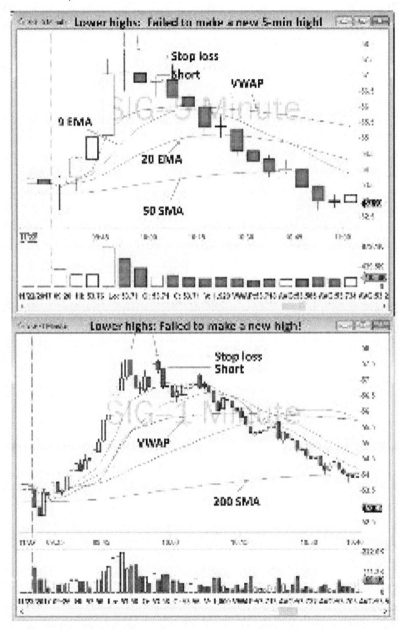

Figure 62 – Shows an Example of the VWAP Reversal on SIG.

The second target profit would have been perfectly placed at the 20 EMA on my 5-minute chart and later on the 50 SMA on my 5-minute chart. This is only of the reasons I have always implored traders to strive to cover the first part of their position at the VWAP, by bring forth the stop loss to create a break-even point and then wait on for the next move. As you would see from this example that, the SIG experienced a sold off from $57 to below $54, around 200 SMA, on my 1-minute chart. In order to expantiate better the importance of positioning several profit targets, we will look at the Figure 63, which was a trade that I was not able to manage decently on the American food and beverage company, which is the largest dairy company in America, Dean Foods Company (ticker: DF). This stock opened quite weak and as a result had to sell off below the VWAP, but was unable to make the recent 5-minute low for on the 5-minute Opening Range Breakout. So i opted to go long at $8.40 and added more share at $8.45 for it to pop above the VWAP. But as I went along with the trade, I got cold feet and had to sell off my positions very early for a small profit, but you would see, that DF was able squeezed right above the VWAP and hit the 9 EMA and 20 EMA. I could not make this trade as rewarding as it should be: Long with price at $8.45 with a sign of a failure to make a recent low on my 5-minute chart

Stop loss was below the low of the day

First target: VWAP was at $8.55

Second target: 9 EMA on my 5-minute chart

Third target: 20 EMA on my 5-minute chart

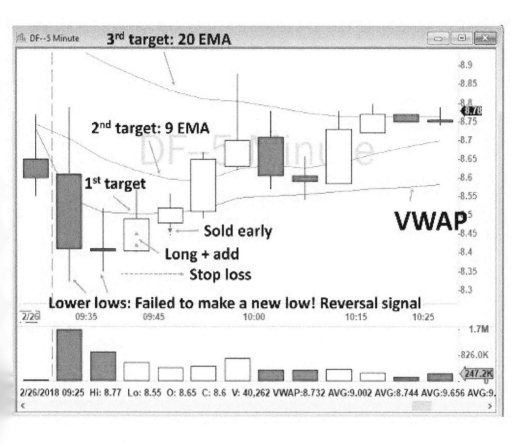

Figure 63 – Shows an Example of DF VWAPon the Reversal with different profit targets postions.

I was not fortunate enough to make the most of this trade and missed the move. As I have previously mentioned, when I went long on the trade, I had a cold feet and was not able to stick to my trading strategies, so I thought selling off my position early was a better choice. This shows another good illustration of VWAP Reversal with different profit targets on the 11th of May, 2018 the trading behavior of the American software company Symantec Corporation (ticker: SYMC), set out in Figure 64. The SYMC stock was unable to make the recent low on my 5-minute chart, as such the stock had to sell off at the Open toward $18.75. This trade only signaled to me a decent opportuinty to go long. So I went long with the trade when price was at $19.21 with my stop loss positioned below the low of the previous 5 minute candles at around $19 with the first profit target of VWAP. My other profit targets were 20 EMA on my 1-minute chart and also 20 EMA on my 5-minute chart. I sold off my position with the stock on the way up. However, the stock was able to break beyond the 20 EMA on my 1-minute chart, but it was not able to reach the 20 EMA on my 5-minute chart. When the stock started to sell off backward toward the VWAP, I had to sell off of my last long postions to cover my profits. I ended the trade with an amazing total profit of $1,539, as it is shown in Figure 64 below.

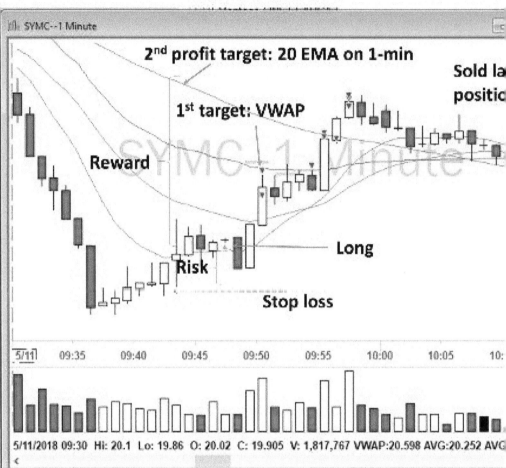

Set the Rules for Exit

One of the main mistakes that most traders fail to understand is that they usually concentrate over 80% of their efforts in trying to look for signals showing buy. They, however, fail to look at where and when they should exit a trade. Most investors will not risk selling if they are down because they are usually not ready for losses. You should get over it or else you will never make it in the trading world. Don't take things personally, especially when you are making losses. It only indicates that your predictions were incorrect. Keep it in mind that professional/experienced traders often have more losing trades that the winning trades. You will still make profits if you are able to manage your investments and limit your loses. Therefore before entering a trade, clearly know yours exists. For every trade you do, ensure that you have at least two exit points. The first exit point is the stop-loss which will tell you to exit in the event that you are trading negatively. You should ensure that you have a written exit spot and not memorizing them. Second, ensure that you have a profit target for each trade you perform. However, don't risk more than the percentage that you have set in your portfolio. Here are exit strategies you can choose;

Exit Strategy: Traditional Stop/Limit

The most effective way to keep your emotions in check is by setting targets or limits and stops the moment a trade is entered into. You can use the DailyFX to research into the over 4o million traders. You will realize that most of the successful traders set their risk to reward ratio to at least 1:1. Before entering into a market, you have to analyze the amount of risk you are willing to assume and then set a stop at this level, while at the same time, place your target at least many pips away. This means that if your predictions were wrong, your trade would be closed automatically, and this will be at an acceptable risk level. If your prediction is correct, the trade will be closed automatically after having your target. In either way, you will still have an exit.

Exit Strategy: Moving Average Trailing Stops

This exit strategy is also referred to as a moving average. This strategy is effective in filtering the direction a currency pair has trended. The main idea behind this strategy is that traders are usually busy looking for buying opportunities, particularly when the prices are above a moving average. Traders will also be busy looking for selling opportunities, especially when the prices are moving below the average. Therefore this strategy also considers the fact that a moving average can also be a trailing stop. This means that if a moving average cross over price, the trend is considered to be shifting. When you are a trend trader, you would consider closing out the position the moment a shift has occurred. It is preferred that you set your stop loss based on a moving average, as this is very effective.

Fig.1: Setting a trade exit using a moving average trailing stops

Exit Strategy: Volatility Bases Approach Using ATR

This technique involves the use of the Average True Range (ATR), which is designed to determine market volatility. It calculates the average range of the last 14 candles found between the high and low and thereby tells a trader the erratic behavior of the market. Traders can, therefore, use this to set stops and limits for every trade they do. A greater ATR on a given pair means a wider stop. This means if a volatile pair can generally be stopped out early, and thus will have a tight stop. You can adopt ATR for any time frame; a factor that makes to be considered as a universal indicator.

Set Entry Rules

We have set the exit rules to come before the entry rules for a reason. The reason is that exits are very important compared to entries. The entry rule is basically simple. For instance, we can have an entry rule like: "Given that signal, B fires up and we have the minimum set target is suggested to be three times the stop loss, from the fact that we give that we at service, buying Y shares or contracts here is appropriated and allowed." In as much as the effectiveness of most of these systems are determined by how complicated they are, it should also be simple enough to enable you to make effective decisions quickly. In many cases, computers usually make better trade decisions than humans and this is the reason why nearly 50% of all trades occurring today are generated on computer programs.

Computers have powerful information processing capabilities and will not want to think or rely on emotions to make decisions. If a given condition is met, then they will automatically enter. They will exit when the trade hits its profit target or when the trade goes the wrong way. Each of the decisions made by a computer is based on probabilities. Otherwise, if you rely alone on your thoughts, it will difficult for you or almost impossible to make trades.

Building an effective watchlist requires three basic steps. The first step is collecting a handful of liquidity components of leadership in each of the major sectors in the market. Secondly, you will scan through stocks that meet the general technical criteria fitting your approach to the stock market. Third, do a rescan on the list nightly to be able to identify and locate setups or patterns that can generate opportunities in the session to follow while at the same time culling out the issues you don't have interest on may be due to their technical violations or secondary offerings, etc.

Building A Watchlist

The U.S stock exchanges, for example, list more than 8,000 issues. However, a fund manager or a typical trader only access just a fraction. Why? because they have failed to come up with their effective watchlists. The main reason behind this failure is because the identification of stocks that can fully support working strategies needs some skill sets, which is usually lacking in most participants. It is therefore wise that you learn this because it will mark a trading edge that is a lifetime. For you to have a well-organized watchlist, you should have a proper understanding of the modern market environment; you need to have an understanding of how different capitalization levels impact on price development. Lastly, you should also understand how different sectors are likely to react to different catalysts over time. When choosing the candidates you want to follow, be it on a daily, weekly, or monthly basis, you have to consider economic cycles, seasonality, and sentiments.

Guidelines for Building a Watchlist

The requirements of a watchlist depend on the amount of time a trader has to do trade and as well follow the financial markets. For instance, if you are a part-timer who only plays a few positions each week, daily, you can have a simple culling list having 50-100 issues to track. Otherwise, if you are a professional trader, you have to spend more time on the task. You should build a primary database containing 350 - 500 stocks. You should also have a secondary list fitting your trading screens. Note that each trading screen should be able to accommodate between 20 and 75 issues, but this will depend on the space that charts, market depth, scanners, and news stickers windows will take. It is appropriate that to trade well, one screen should be devoted to stickers and each entry of these stickers should display just a maximum of three fields like the percentage change, the last price, and the net change. Try to link these stickers as this will enable you to have a quick review of price patterns, particularly during the trading day.

Execution

This refers to the completion of a sell or buys of an order for a security. Order execution occurs when the order gets filled and not when an order is placed by an investor. As an investor, when you submit the trade, the trade is sent to a broker. The broker determines the best way with which this trade can be executed. The law requires that brokers give the best execution possible to the investors. There is an established commission, referred to as the Securities and Exchange Commission, where brokers report the quality of their executions. Brokers are also required to notify customers whose orders were not routed for best execution. The growth of online brokers today has made the cost of trade execution to reduce significantly. Today, many traders offer a commission rebate to their customers for some set monthly targets for these customers. This can be very important for the short-term trader who tries to keep the execution costs low as possible.

There are high probabilities that you will be able to settle at the desired price if you have placed a market order or any other order that is relatively easy to be converted into a market order. However, this does not apply for all cases because there are orders that may be too large and will require that they be broken down to come up with several small orders and this might be very difficult to execute and get the best possible price range. To solve this, you can involve the use of risk in the system. Execution risk is the lag between order placement and settlement.

How Did I Do It?

Trading is a business and for you to succeed in trading, you have to treat it just the same way you would have treated any other business. As a trader, all does not stop with having knowledge on where the market has the potential to rise or fall or when to pause or reverse but rather a trader must be able to precisely determine what exact market event is going to take place and act accordingly. While trading, you have a well-written plan that is subjected to re-evaluation after the closing of a market. Your plan must be able to change with the changing market conditions. So be an individual who can adjust and improve your trading skills. Just like we have discussed in the previous sections, your plan as a trader should take into account your personal trading goals and styles. Never use another person's trading plan as this will not reflect your characteristics. A successful trade must begin by building a perfect master plant. A good trading plan will include the following;

Skill Assessment

Begin by first assessing your skills so you know whether you are ready to trade or not. Try to test your trading system by doing trading on paper and determine if you are confident that it will work. Check if you can follow your signals without any hesitation. You must have a clear mentality that trading in stock markets is like being on a battlefield that involves giving away or taking. Professional traders are always well prepared and they are ready to take profits and earn interests from those who do not have a plan and mostly give away their money as a result of their costly mistakes.

Be Mentally Prepared

Assess yourself and check how you feel, are you able to get good sleep at night? Are you feeling pressured by the challenge ahead? It is usually advised that when you are not psychologically, physically and emotionally prepared for the battle in the markets, just keep off because you are at high risk of losing your investments. This mostly happens when you get angry and act out of emotions. In many situations, traders have a market mantra that gets them ready before a day begins. It is appropriate that you create the market mantra that will always put you in a safer trading zone. Ensure that your stock trading areas are free from interruptions and distractions because, in any business, distractions are always costly.

Set Your Risk Levels

Ask yourself the risk you can handle in any trade you make. However, this is determined by your risk tolerance and trading style. On any given trading day, your portfolio should have a risk tolerance ranging between 1% - 5%. This means that on any trading day, if you happen to lose an amount that is in that range, you will get out of the trade. It is always better to fight another day.

Set Goals

An effective trader sets realistic profit targets before entering any trade. You have to assess the minimum risk/reward ratios you can accept. As observed, most pro traders will always not accept to take a trade unless the potential profit that the trade will yield is at least twice or thrice the risk. A good scenario is a case where you have a dollar loss per share in your stop-loss; therefore, your goal will be making a $3 profit. Be precise; ensure that you set your weekly, monthly and at large your annual profit goal either in as a percentage or in dollars of your trade portfolio. Regularly re-assess these goals.

Do Your At-Home Research

A trader is always informed and up to date person. Before the market opens, always ensure that you have gone through news and other sources to read what are the current trends in the world. Check whether the overseas stock and forex markets are down or up. Check whether index futures like the S&P 500 to know if they are down or up in the pre-market. The index features will provide you with the best ways to gauge the mood of the market before the opening of the market. Also, check through to know the earnings or economic data that are due. It is appropriate that you create a list that will guide you in deciding whether you would like to trade ahead of an important report or not. We prefer that you avoid taking unnecessary risks and wait for the release of the report. Pro traders don't gamble but rather they trade based on probabilities.

Trade Preparation

Always label the minor and major resistance and support levels regardless of the trading program or system you are using. Ensure that your plan also contains signals for entering and exiting a trade. Your signals should be easily detected (clear visual signal) or detected (clear auditory signal).

Always Keep Excellent Records

Professional traders keep clear records. They are interested in knowing why they won or lost a trade so that they will not make the same mistakes they made when they lost. Always ensure that you write down details like your entry and exit, goals, targets, time, market open and close, resistance and support levels and daily opening range. Always keep a record of comments on why you made a particular trade and the potential lessons you learned. Keeping trading records will help you to analyze your profits and losses for a given system; you will also be able to determine the amounts you lost per trade when you used a particular trade system. You will learn the average time you took per trade with will enable you to calculate the trade efficiency.

CHAPTER 9
Understanding Trading Orders

As a trader, you will need a broker through whom you will place buy or sell orders for any asset. You can decide whether you are going to buy or sell any stock, then place an order accordingly on your online trading platform.

Usually, Exchanges use a bid and ask process for fulfilling orders placed by traders. This means that there must be a buyer and seller to complete a single order, and they both should agree on the price. For example, if a trader wants to buy a stock at X price, there must be a seller willing to sell that stock at the same price. No transaction can occur unless a buyer and a seller agree at the same price.

The bid is the highest price a trader is willing to pay to buy an asset, and the ask is the lowest price, that trader is willing to accept to sell that asset. In stock markets, the price moment is directed by a tussle between the bid and ask prices. These prices keep constantly changing. As trading orders get filled, the price levels also keep changing, which is reflected in the technical charts.

While day trading, one must keep in mind this bid and ask process, because this will determine at what price the order will be executed. When markets are moving slowly, the change in price is also slow and one can wait to get the trading orders filled at the desired price. However; when markets are highly volatile and sees big up or down moves happen within split seconds, the order may get filled on a higher than expected rate. This can cause losses to day traders as the price changes quickly and can reverse by the time their orders are filled.

Different markets have different methods of matching buyers' and sellers' prices. These methods are called trading mechanisms. There are two main types of trading mechanisms; order-driven, and quote driven. In markets that use quote driven trading, a constant stream of prices (quotes) is available to traders. These prices are decided by market makers, therefore; these types of trading systems are better suited for over the counter (OTC) markets or dealers. There is a considerable spread between the bid and ask prices, which constitutes the profit of the deal maker or the market maker.

Exchanges mostly adopt the order-driven trading mechanism. Here, orders are executed when buy orders match with a sell order. In this type of trading mechanism, dealmakers are not involved.

Mechanism of Trading Orders

In the electronic day trading, orders are placed on the online trading platforms. These orders are the trader's instructions to the broker, or the brokerage firm, for buying or selling some security. When you are trading stocks, you place orders to buy or sell a stock, which is fulfilled by the brokerage firm with whom you have a trading account. The ease of electronic trading has given traders the freedom to initiate various types of order, where they can use different restrictions in order conditions. By these restrictions, traders can control the price and time of order execution. Such instructions help increase traders' profits or restrict the losses.

In systems, where the trading mechanism is order-driven, traders can also control the timeline of any specific order. For example, a trader can place an order which will remain open until its execution. Traders can also place orders that last till the end of the session, or one day, or a specific time.

Understanding how trading orders are placed, and how they can impact one's day trading, is important because it can affect once profit or loss in day trading. For example, a novice day trader may not be aware of the slippage between the bid and ask prices. There is always a difference between the bid and ask price is called slippage. It occurs in every trade, and every trader faces it whether buying, selling, entering a position or exiting from a position. This is also called the spread between a bid and ask price. So, when you place an order to buy a stock at $4, the slippage may increase its cost to $4.05 when your order is filled. Likewise; when you are existing any position, you place an order to sell at $3, but the slippage causes it to get filled at $2.98, thus chipping away at some of your profits.

Professional traders advise beginners to stay away from highly volatile market situations because the slippage risk increases during those choppy moments. For example; on a central bank policy declaration day, stock prices become highly volatile and move with big numbers within seconds. In such a situation, the ordered price and executed price may be different, causing financial harm to the day trader. From the outside, such big moves may look tempting to day traders and make them greedy, thinking they can make big profits with such huge price moves. But the reality is, the slippage between the bid and ask price is equally big and it can change considerably by the time the trading order gets filled, or immediately after the order is executed, creating a loss-making situation for the trader.

Different Types of Trading Orders

Most individual traders use a broker or dealers' trading platforms to place their trading orders. These platforms provide the facility of placing various types of orders, which are helpful in trade planning. Placing an order on the trading platforms is instructing the brokerage firm to buy or sell a financial asset on behalf of the trader. Based on the execution type, here are some common order types:

Market Orders: These orders do not have any specific price. A market order is an instruction to the broker to complete the trade at the available price. Because there is no fixed price, these orders almost always get executed, unless there is some liquidity problem. Traders use market orders when they want their trades executed quickly and they are not bothered about the execution price.

These orders are good if there is not much slippage between the bid and ask price. But a big slippage can cause loss to the traders, especially those who day trade in options.

Limit Orders: Traders place limit orders when they want to buy or sell stocks (or other assets) at a specific price. For example, if Apple shares are trading at $220, and traders expect the price to dip low, they can place a limit order to buy the shares at $219 or lower. Limit orders can be used for both buying and selling. Traders use these orders when they are trading with technical levels and are sure of price touching those level. For example, if a trader has bought Apple shares at $220, and thinks it can touch $222, he can place a limit order to sell his shares at that higher price. When the share price reaches that level, his sell order will get executed.

Stop Orders: These are also known as stop-loss orders and make a part of traders' money management techniques. A stop-loss order can stop the trade from going below a specific price, thus restricting losses for the trader. These orders are used for both buy and sell trades. The price specified in a stop-loss order is called stop price; and once that price is reached, the order is executed as a market order.

Day Order: This order Is valid only in the same trading session where it is placed. If the specified price is not achieved by the end of the session, the order is automatically canceled. This saves day traders from carrying forward their orders to the next day.

Preparations for Placing an Order

When preparing day trading plans and strategies, many day traders forget to pay attention that how they will place orders for trades. Believe it or not, the simple act of placing a trading order can have a big impact on the success of your day trading business.

Successful day traders always give importance to order processing techniques and plan their trades around the stock price they will focus during the trading. The trading plan itself means planning at what price you will enter a trade and when you will exit. Online trading platforms provide many methods of placing your orders around your planned trade prices. You can prepare charts of your trade, mark entry, and exit points and place orders for both trades together, or separately.

A good trading plan always includes trade entry, exit, profit booking, and loss stopping points. The margin trading facility provided by various brokerage firms also includes placing a stop-loss order together with the primary buy or sell order. This ensures that your trade will never suffer a loss beyond a specific price level. Here is an example to illustrate this:

Suppose a trader has bought stock 'A' at $10. He is expecting the price to go up, so he'll make some profit. However; anything can happen in stock markets and in case the price reverses, he wants to restrict his losses to $3 only. So, he will place a stop-loss order at $7, which is $3 below his buying price. If the price keeps moving up, the stop loss order will remain inactive. In case, the stock price falls, nothing will happen till it reaches $7, at which time the stop loss order will be triggered, and automatically sell the stock he has bought.

A stop-loss order makes sure that even if the trader is not available to check prices, his position will be safe till a certain price.

Similarly, traders can also use limit orders to exit their positions after earning a profit. Taking the above example once again, if a trader has bought a stock at $10, and believes that the price will move up to $15; he can place a limit order to sell at $15. When the price reaches his target ($15), it will be automatically executed, and the position will be squared off with a profit of $5.

These examples show that day traders can use a combination of different order types for money management and managing the risk and reward ratio. By technical analysis of any stock chart, day traders can find at what price the stock will make a big move, and be ready to place their orders near that price level.

Some other Order Types:

Apart from the basic orders, some other order types are not so common but can be used for money management or specific trading strategies.

For example, some day traders are more active during the market closing hours, as they create trading strategies for the next session. To take advantage of the price movement during the closing hours, they can place 'Limit-On-Close' (LOC) orders. As the name shows, it is a limit order and is specified for getting executed when markets close. As you know, a limit order controls at what price any security will be bought or sold. LOC has an extra parameter of 'on close', which adds another condition to this order, that it should only get executed if the closing price matches the order's price limit. For this order, both the limit price and the market's closing price are important.

Expert day traders use this order to take advantage of the closing time volatility in the stock markets, where they expect the price to reach a certain level. The LOC order has a drawback; if the closing price does not reach the limit price of the order, it is not executed. Also, this order must be placed within a specific time, before markets close for the day. The LOC order is valid only through the same trading session and is not carried forward to the next session.

Sometimes when the trader places this order but its requirements are not met for a while, the trader decides to wait till it gets executed. In that situation, it will be called an open order. The order will remain open until the trader does not actively cancel it. All open day orders get canceled automatically at the end of the session. During the session. If traders do not wish to wait further for the trade to take place, they will have to cancel all open orders manually. The open orders are often caused by buying or sell limit orders or stop orders. Traders can use GTC (good till canceled) option for their open orders, which will carry forward their orders until it is executed. Traders have the option to cancel the open order at any time.

When traders open any order and then decide not to get it executed, they can cancel it and it becomes a canceled order. This can happen when they mistakenly place a wrong order and upon realizing their mistake, immediately cancel the order. Or sometimes, they place a limit order, wait for it to get executed, then decide not to complete the trade and cancel the order. Market orders usually get immediately executed, so it is difficult to cancel a market order after it has been placed. But limit and stop orders have a time gap before getting executed. Therefore; traders can cancel these orders before their execution.

For stock trading, one needs to place buy or sell orders through a broker. There must be a buyer and seller to complete any order and they should agree on a specific price to complete the trade. Stock prices move through a process of the bid and ask. Day traders must keep this in mind when they are placing an order because the difference between the bid and ask price can cause slippage, which is harmful to a day traders' profits. Different markets have a different trading mechanism.

Online trading platforms facilitate order execution. Traders place their orders through the platform, which is executed by the brokerage firm. The time and method of order placing can impact one's day trading profits and losses. The spread or the difference between the bid and ask price can change at what price any trade is executed. Therefore; beginner day traders should stay away from volatile markets because, in those market conditions, the slippages can cause them considerable financial harm.

Day traders can use different order types to execute the trade. Market orders are executed almost immediately at the latest available price. These orders are good to use when markets are trending. Most of the time, day traders prefer to place limit orders where they can control the buy or sell price of their trades. Traders also used stop-orders to control the loss or to decide the profit booking levels in their trades. For intraday trading, traders can use the day order, which, if not fulfilled, gets canceled at the end of the session.

Order placing has an important place in traders' money management and trading strategies. Traders can pre-plan their trades and decide at what level they will buy or sell any stock. Technical analysis can help them find levels where the stock price will make considerable moments. They can place different orders near these price levels to manage their trades. Day traders can combine various orders to manage their risk and reward ratio.

Apart from the basic order types, there are many other orders, which expert traders use for their trading strategies. LOC or 'Limit-On-Close' Is one such order that traders can use to buy or sell stocks at the market-closing price. They can use this order type to take advantage of the closing hours' high volatility in markets, or if they are planning any strategy for the next day's opening session. Any order that is not filled is called an open order. Sometimes traders cancel their orders for various reasons, and these are called canceled orders.

CHAPTER 10
Money Mistake to avoid

Now we'll turn our attention to giving some tips, tricks and advice on errors to avoid in order to ensure as much as possible that you have a successful time trading.

Avoid The Get Rich Quick Mentality

Any time that people get involved with trading or investing, the hope is always there that there's a possibility of the big winning trade. It does happen now and then. But quite frankly, it's a rare event. In many occasions, even experienced traders are guessing wrong and taking losses. It's important to approach Forex for what it really is. It's a business. It is not a gambling casino even though a lot of people treated that way so you need to come to your Forex business—and it is a business no matter if you do it part-time, or quit your job and devote your entire life to it—with the utmost seriousness. You wouldn't open a restaurant and recklessly buy 1 thousand pounds of lobster without seeing if customers were coming first. So, why would you approach Forex as if you were playing slots at the casino? Take it seriously and act as if it's a business because it really is. Again, it doesn't matter if you officially create a corporation to do your trades or not, it's still a business no matter what. That means you should approach things with care and avoid the get rich quick mentality. The fact is the get rich quick mentality never works anywhere. Unfortunately, I guess I could say I've been too strong in my assertion. It does work on rare occasions. It works well enough that it keeps the myth alive. But if we took 100 Forex traders who have to get rich quick mentality, my bet is within 90 days, 95% of them would be completely broke.

Trade Small

You should always trade small and set small achievable goals for your trading. The first benefit to trading small is that this approach will help you avoid a margin call. Second, it will also help you set profit goals that are small and achievable. That will help you stay in business longer.

Simply put, you will start gaining confidence and learning how to trade effectively if you get some trades that make $50 profits, rather than shooting for a couple of trades that would make thousands of dollars in one shot, but and up making you completely broke. Again, treat your trading like a real business. If you were opening a business, chances are you would start looking for slow and steady improvements and you certainly would not hope to get rich quick.

Let's get specific. Trading small means never trading standard lots. Even if you have enough cash to open an account such that you could trade standard lots, I highly recommend that you stay away from them. The large amount of capital involved and margin that would be used could just get you into a lot of financial trouble. For beginners, no matter how much money you are able to devote to your trading, I recommend that you start with micro lots. Take some time and learn how to trade with the small lots and start building your business earnings small profits at a time. Trading only with micro lots will help in force discipline and help you avoid getting into trouble. Make a commitment only to use micros for the first 60 days. After that, if you have been having decent success, consider trading a mini lot. You should be extremely cautious for the first 90 days in general.

Be Careful With Leverage

Obviously, it's extremely beneficial. It allows you to enter and trades that would otherwise not be possible. On the other hand, the temptation is there to use all your leverage in the hopes of making it big on one or two trades. You need to avoid using up all your leverage. Remember that you can have a margin call and get yourself into big trouble if your trades go bad.

And it's important to remember there's a high probability that some of your trades are going to go bad no matter how carefully you do all your analysis.

Not Using A Demo Account

A big mistake the beginners make, is jumping in too quickly. There is a reason that most broker-dealers provide demos or simulated accounts. If you don't have a clue what that reason is, let's go ahead and stated here. Brokers provide demo accounts because Forex is a high-risk trading activity. It can definitely be something that provides a lot of rewards and it does for large numbers of traders. But there is a substantial risk of losing your capital. Many beginners are impatient hoping to make money right away. That's certainly understandable, but you don't want to fall into that trap. Take 30 days to practice with a demo account. This will provide several advantages. Trading on Forex is different than trading on the stock market. Using the demo account, you can become familiar with all the nuances of Forex trading. This includes everything from studying the charts, to placing your orders and, most importantly, understanding both pips and margin. The fact that there is so much leverage available means you need to learn how to use it responsibly. You need to know how to experience going through the process and reading the available margin and so forth on your trading platform while you are actually trying to execute trades. A demo account let you do this without risking real capital. It is true that it's not a perfect simulation. The biggest argument against demo accounts is that they don't incorporate the emotion that comes with trading and real money. As we all know, it's those emotions, including panic, fear and greed, that lead to bad decisions. However, in my opinion, that is a weak argument against using demo accounts. The proper way to approach it is to use a demo account for 30 days and then spend 60 to 90 days doing nothing but trading micro lots. Don't worry, as your micro trading lots you can increase the number of your trades and earn profits. While I know you're anxious to get started, keeping yourself from losing all your money is a good reason to practice for 30 days before doing it for real.

Failing To Check Multiple Indicators

There is also a temptation to get into trades quickly just on a gut level hunch. You need to avoid this approach at all costs. Some beginners will start learning about candlesticks and then when they first start trading, they will recognize a pattern on a chart. Then in the midst of the excitement, they will enter a large trade based on what they saw. And then they will end up on the losing end of a trade. Some people are even worse and they don't even look at the candlesticks. Instead, they just look at the trend and think they better get in on it and they got all anxious about doing so. That means first checking the candlesticks and then confirming at least with the moving average before entering or exiting a position. You should also have the RSI handy and you may or may not want to use Bollinger bands.

Use Stop Loss And Take Profit Orders

Well, I hate to repeat myself yet again, but this point is extremely important. I am emphasizing it over and over because it's one of the tools that you can use in order to protect yourself from heavy losses. One of the ways that you can get out of having to worry about margin calls and running out of money is to put stop-loss orders every time you trade. This will require studying the charts more carefully. You need to have a very clear idea where you want to get out of the trade, if it doesn't go in the direction you hoped. But if you have a stop-loss order in place, then you can avoid the problem of having your account just go down the toilet. Secondly, although the temptation is always there to look for as many profits as possible, in most cases, you should opt to set a take profit order when you make your trade. That way you set as we said, distinct boundaries which will ensure that you make some profit without taking too much risk. The problem with doing it manually is that excitement and greed will put you in a position where are you miss the boat entirely. What inevitably happens, is people get too excited hoping to earn more profits and they stay in the trade too long. The Forex market changes very fast and so what eventually happens is people that stay into long inevitably and up with a loss. Or at the very least they end up missing out on profits.

There is one exception to this point. There are some times when there is a distinct and relatively long-term upward trend. If you find yourself, by doing the analysis and determining that such an upward trend is here, that might be an exception to the rule. In that case you want to try to ride the trend and maximize your profits.

Remember Price Changes Are In Pips

Beginners often make the mistake of forgetting about pips. If you have trouble with pips and converting them to actual money, go back and review the examples we provided. Remember that pips play a central role in price changes, you need to know your dollar value per pip in order to keep tabs on your profit and losses. This is also important for knowing the right stop loss and take profit orders to execute.

Don't Try Too Many Strategies Or Trading Styles At Once

When you are a beginning Forex trader, it can be tempting to try everything under the sun. That can be too much for a lot of people. The most advisable thing to do is to stick with one strategy so don't try scalping and being a position trader at the same time. The shorter the time frame for your trades, the more time and energy, you have to put into each trade. Scalping and day trading are activities that would require full-time devotion. They are also high-pressure and that can help enhance emotions involved in the trades. For that reason, I don't really recommend those styles or strategies for beginners. In my opinion and to be honest it's mine alone, I think position trading is also too much for a beginner. It requires too much patience.

Perhaps the best strategy to use when you're beginning Forex trading is to become a swing trader. It's a nice middle ground, in between the most extremely active trading styles and something that is going to try people's patience such as position trading. When you do swing trading, you can do time periods longer than a day certainly, but as long or short as you need to meet your goals otherwise. Swing trading also takes off some of the pressure. And it gives you more time to think and react.

This does not mean that you can't become a scalper or day trader at some future date. What I am advising is that you gain some experience using more relaxed trading styles before taking that path. And believe me, swing trading is going to be challenging enough.

Market Expectations

Life as a forex trader can sometimes get lonely. After all, this is the kind of career where you are completely on your own. You enjoy your profits alone, but you also suffer losses on your own. There is no one in the forex market whom you can depend on to comfort you. Therefore, it is also good if you connect with like-minded people. Feel free to make friends with other traders. After all, you are all players in the market who want the same thing. The good thing is that you are not competing with one another. In fact, you can even help one another by sharing information, insights, and strategies. Thanks to the Internet, it is very easy to find and connect with people who are also interested in forex trading. You simply have to join an online group or forum on forex trading. You can do this quickly with just a few clicks of a mouse. You can then make a public post or even send a private message to any member of the group/forum. If you have a neighbor or friend who also likes trading currencies, then you can invite him out for a coffee one of these days. Connecting with like-minded people is not just a way to learn but it can also inspire you to become a better trader.

- Have fun

Forex trading is fun. This is a fact. In fact, many traders get to enjoy this kind of life that they still continue to learn it despite their losses. It is also not uncommon to find traders, especially beginners, who spend their whole day just learning about forex trading. Like gambling in a casino, trading currencies can also be very addicting, especially if you are making a nice profit from it.

Learn to have fun and enjoy the journey. Sometimes taking things too seriously can ruin the experience and even make you less effective. In your life as a trader, you will definitely make some mistakes from time to time. You will experience losing money from what otherwise would have been a profitable trade if only you knew better. Do not get too stressed. The important thing is for you to learn as much as you can from every mistake. Take it easy, but remember to learn from the experience. Making mistakes is part of the learning process. Of course, you should try to minimize them as much as possible. Learn and have fun.

Risk Management

Risks do occur in every sphere of life. However, when it comes to trading in forex securities, these risks, more so, financial risks are enhanced. This is due to the volatility of the foreign exchange currencies.

Nature of Forex risk

Forex risk (currency risk, FX risk or exchange rate risk) is a risk (financial) that prevails when a financial transaction is monetized in a foreign currency. When it comes to multinationals, forex risk occurs when one or several of its subsidiaries maintain financial records and statements in currencies other than those of the parent entity. When it comes to a multinational, there is a risk that there could be negative movements in foreign currency of the subsidiary entities in relation to the domestic currency of the parent entity prior to the report being compiled. International traders are also exposed to this risk.

Types of forex risks

There are many types of forex risks. Nonetheless, the following are the major types of forex risk:

- Transaction risk – This occurs where a firm has cash commitments whose values are subject to unforeseeable changes in exchange rate due to a contract being considered in foreign currency. The cash commitments may include account receivables and account payables.
- Economic risk – A firm is exposed to economic risk when its market value is susceptible to unanticipated changes in forex rate. This may affect the firm's share value, present and future values of cash flows, firm's market position and ultimately firm's overall value.

153

- Translation risk – Translation risk affects mainly multinational firms. Thus, a firm's translation risk is the susceptibility of its financial statements and reports to forex changes. This happens when a parent firm has to prepare consolidated statements, including those of its foreign subsidiaries. This largely affects the firms reported income. This also affects its stock value in the securities market.
- Contingent risk – Contingent risks occurs when a firm engages in foreign contracts thus resulting in foreign-denominated obligations. Such foreign contracts may include bidding for foreign projects, commitments to foreign direct investment (for example, investing in foreign subsidiaries), and settling legal disputes involving foreign entities.

CHAPTER 11
Forex risk management

Several strategies exist to safeguard against forex risks. Some of these strategies include:

- Forex hedging strategies – This covers transaction exposure. Use of money market tools and derivatives can help reduce these risks. Futures contracts, options, forward contracts, and swaps are some of these derivatives. Some operational techniques to support these strategies include payments and exposure netting, leading and lagging of receipts, and currency invoicing.
- Translation exposure strategies - These are strategies aimed at risks that are primarily due to prevailing reporting standard (or differences in reporting standards between the parent company and its foreign subsidiaries), which mainly affect the net assets and net liabilities. This can be mitigated through hedging the balance sheet. In this regard, a firm can purchase a commensurate amount of exposed assets or liabilities to balance off any discrepancy due to forex rates. A business entity can also hedge against translation exposure by using Forex derivatives.
- Alternative strategies to manage economic or operating exposure can also be adopted. This may involve carefully selecting production sites with a clear intent to cut down on production cost, flexible approach to sourcing of supplies on the international markets, diversification in the export market. Creating product differentiation through extensive research and development can also help in hedging against economic risks.

Forex risk management tools and techniques

Several tools and techniques that you can employ in the forex risk management. These tools and techniques include:

Forward Contract

- Limit Orders
- Stop Loss Orders

Options

Forward contract

A forward contract allows a user to hedge expected forex transactions by locking in a price today for a transaction that will take place in future. This enables the trader to eliminate or mitigate risks of exchange rate fluctuations. Forward contracts can last for as long as a year.

Limit Orders

You can use Limit Orders in transactions that do not have time-restricted payment obligations. Thus, a business can set an ideal exchange rate at which to buy a particular currency. For example, if the current exchange rate is EUR/0.72GBP, a businessperson may not wish to send £50,000 to the UK until he can get a better rate. He can make a limit order to his payment provider target a rate of EUR/0.75GBP. When this rate is attained, a transfer is triggered, and funds are automatically sent to the UK.

Stop Loss Orders

Stop loss orders guarantees a minimum rate at which a currency is exchanged by allowing a trader to lock in a deal so that it never trades below what he considers as an acceptable exchange rate. It is, in essence, an instruction to buy or sell a currency at a predetermined 'worst case' exchange rate.

Options

An option is a risk management tool in forex transactions. It protects businesses from downturns in the currency market, but also allows them to take advantage of positive currency shifts. When a business buys an option it secures the right, but not the obligation, to make an international purchase or exchange funds at a predetermined exchange rate on a chosen date. Where Options differ to FECs is that the buyer is not obligated to settle on that date. If movements in the forex market present more favorable exchange rates than the rate that was set when the Option was bought, the buyer is not obliged to settle.

Tips and hacks on risk management:

Set Orders – Limit orders, stop orders, trail orders, etc

- Set risk/reward ratio
- Set win-rate

Blend win-rate and risk/reward ratio to derive the most optimal strategy

Focus less on short-term performance targets and more on mid-term and long-term performance targets

Carry out position sizing

- Blend R-Multiple with Risk/Reward ratio to balance between performance and potential

Make spread vs. fees comparison for net profit

- Watch out for correlations – pairs that are positively correlated increase your risks

BACKTESTING

Backtesting is the process of testing your trading strategy on previous historical data to establish its efficacy and reliability in as far as establishing how accurately the strategy would have predicted the actual result. Thus, if the strategy works on historical data, then, it is expected to work on the current and future data.

Why carry out Backtesting?

The following are some of the important reasons as to why you need to carry out Backtesting:

- To test the efficacy and reliability of your trading strategy.
- To iron out flaws in your strategy so as to improve its efficacy and reliability.
- To cut down on risks that would arise due to unreliable strategy.
- To have an insight into how your intended forex system is going to work.
- To refine your trading strategy parameters.

Types of Backtesting

There are two main types of backtesting:

Manual backtesting.

- Automated backtesting.

Manual backtesting

In manual backtesting, you largely design your own testing system. You manually enter and exit the markets.

Advantages

You can have the look and feel of your system as you enter and exit the market. You can easily customize the system to your unique needs.

Disadvantages

- Time consuming.
- Reliability is not guaranteed.

Automated backtesting

In automated backtesting, you create a system that automatically enters or exits the market on your behalf. You take advantage of the already existing backtesting systems in the market.

Advantages

- Less susceptible to your emotions
- Automate income generation`

Disadvantages

- A slight error in your coding can cost you heavily
- You have to master the parameters of the system to be able to do a thorough diagnosis should it malfunction

Backtesting tools

Each type of backtesting has its own tools that you can take advantage of:

Manual backtesting tools

- Forex Tester 2
- MetaTrader 4
- TradingView

With MetaTrader 4 and TradingView, you would need to use a spreadsheet program to track your trades. When it comes to analysis of your backtesting results, you can use the following tools:

- MetaTrader4 Reports
- Tradingrex
- Excel

Automated backtesting tools

- MetaTrader MLQ5
- TradingView (pine scripting language)
- TradeStation
- CandleScanner
- QuantShare

Stop Loss And Trailing Stop Loss

In this section, we will delve into more details about these very important risks management tools.

Stop loss

A stop-loss is an Order to buy or sell a forex currency once its price goes higher than or lower than a set stop price. Upon attaining the stop price, the stop order transforms into either a limit order (with a fixed or pre-determined price) or a market order (with no price limit). The stop order, once placed, is automatically triggered.

Without a price limit (market order, thus prevailing market price), the price at which the trade is executed may be different from that of the stop price (either higher or lower). This boosts chance of the trade being executed. However, at higher risk of selling lower than the stop price.

With a limit order, the trade must be executed at a certain pre-determined price or it lapses. This is because there could be lack of buyers or sellers willing to trade at the pre-determined price. It is less risky compared to a market order. However, it has lower chances of being executed compared to a market order.

Different kinds of Stop Loss Orders

1) Stop Loss Market Order

This is an order placed by a business entity to buy a security once its price goes higher than certain specified stop price or to sell a security once its price falls below the set stop price. In this regard, the trader has no control over the price at which the security will be sold. There are two types of Stop Loss Market Order:

- Sell Stop market order – This is an order placed by a seller to sell at the best market price after the price falls below the stop price. It is an order to minimize losses when the seller suspects that the price is on a falling trend. Thus, the seller is able to sell a security before the price goes too low.

- A buy stop market order – This is an order placed by a buyer to buy at the best market price after the price rises above the stop price. It is an order to minimize losses when the buyer suspects that the prices are on a rising trend. Thus, the buyer is able to purchase a security before the price gets too high.

2) Stop Loss Limit Order

This is an order placed by a business entity to purchase a security at no more than or sell a security at no less than a certain fixed price (limit price). There are two types of stop-loss limit orders:

- Stop-loss buy limit order – This is an order placed by a buyer. It can only be executed at the limit price or lower.
- Stop loss sell limit order – This is an order placed by a seller, which gets transacted at the limit price or higher.

Trailing Stop Loss

A trailing stop-loss order, also known as trailing stop-on-quote order, is a stop order where the stop price automatically adjusts by a given point amount or a given percentage. Thus, the stop price automatically adjusts based on the last price of a security under consideration. For a sell order, the execution is triggered by the bid price, while, for buy orders, the execution is triggered by the ask price. Upon trigger by the stop price, a market order (to buy or sell) is sent to the market.

There are two types of trailing stop-loss orders:

- Trailing stop-loss sell order – When the difference between the security's last price and trigger price exceeds the trailing stop amount, then the trigger price is adjusted. The new trigger price will then be established by subtracting the trail stop amount from the security's last price.
- Trailing stop-loss buy order – When the difference between the security's last price and trigger price exceeds the trailing stop amount, then the trigger price get adjusted. The new trigger price will be established by adding the trail stop amount to the last price.

CHAPTER 12
Risk Management Techniques

When people think of day trading, they only think of potential profits, not losses. Therefore, day trading attracts so many people, they don't see the risk of losses. In stock markets, various events can trigger losses for investors and traders, which are beyond their control. These events can be economic conditions such as recession, geopolitical changes, changes in the central bank policies, natural disasters, or sometimes terror attacks.

This is the market risk; the potential of losing money due to unknown and sudden factors. These factors affect the overall performance of stock markets, and regardless of how careful one is while day trading, the possibility of market risk is always present, which can cause losses. The market risk is known as the systematic risk because it influences the entire stock market. There is also a nonsystematic risk, which affects only a specific industry or company. Long-term investors tackle this risk by diversification in their investment portfolio.

Unlike investors, day traders have no method to neutralize market risk, but they can avoid it by keeping track of financial and business events, news, and economic calendars. For example, stock markets are very sensitive to the central banks' rate policies and become highly volatile on those days. Nobody knows what kind of policy any central bank will adopt in its monetary meeting. But day traders can check the economic calendar and know which day these meetings will take place. They can avoid trading on those days and reduce the risk of loss in trading.

Therefore, knowledge of stock markets and being aware of what is happening in the financial world is essential for day traders. Many successful traders have a policy of staying away from trading on days when any major economic event will take place, or a major decision will be announced. For example, on the day when the result of an important election is declared; any big company's court case decision comes in, or a central banks' policy meeting takes place. On such days, speculative trading dominates stock markets and market risk is very high. Similarly, on a day when any company announces earnings results, its stock price fluctuates wildly, increasing the market risk in trading of that stock.

In day trading, there is always a risk that you will lose money. Now, if you want to start day trading as a career, learn a few techniques that will reduce and manage the risk of potential losses. By taking steps to manage the risk, you reduce the potential day trading losses.

To stay in the day trading business for the long term, you must protect your trading capital. By reducing the risk of losses, you open the possibilities of future profits and a sustainable day trading business.

If you plan well, prepare your trading strategies before starting to trade; you increase the possibility of a stable trading practice which can lead to profits. Therefore, it is essential to prepare your trading plans every day, create trading strategies and follow your trading rules. These three things can make or break your day trading business. Professional day traders always plan their trades first and then trade their plans. This can be understood by an example of two imaginary traders. Suppose there are two traders, trading in the same stock market, trading the same stock. One of them has prepared his trading plan and knows when and how he will trade. The other trader has done no planning and is just sitting there, taking the on-the-spot decisions for buying or selling the stock. Who do you think will be more successful? The one who is well prepared, or the one who has no inkling of what he will do the next second?

The second risk management technique is using stop orders. Use these orders to decide to fix your stop -loss and profit booking points, which will take emotions out of your decision-making process, and automatically cut the losses or book the profit for you.

Many a time, profitable trade turns into loss-making because markets change their trend, but traders do not exit their positions, hoping to increase profits. Therefore, it is necessary to keep a profit booking point and exit the profitable trades at that point. Keeping a fix profit booking point can also help you calculate your returns with every trade and help you avoid taking the unnecessary risk for further trades.

Taking emotions out of day trading is a very important requirement for profitable trading. Do not prejudge the trend in stock markets, which many day traders do and trade against markets, ending with losses.

Using Risk-Reward Ratio

Day trading is done for financial rewards and the good thing is, you can always calculate how much risk you take on every trade and how much reward you can expect. The risk-reward ratio represents the expected reward and expected risk traders can earn on the investment of every dollar.

The risk-reward ratio can excellently indicate your potential profits and potential loss, which can help you in managing your investment capital. For example, a trade with the risk-reward ratio of 1:4 shows that at the risk of $1, the trade has the potential of returning $4. Professional traders advise not to take any trade which has a risk-reward ratio lower than 1:3. This indicates, the trader can expect the investment to be $1, and the potential profit $3.

Expert traders use this method for planning which trade will be more profitable and take only those trades. Technical charting is a good technique to decide the risk-reward ratio of any trade by plotting the price moment from support to resistance levels. For example, if a stock has a support level at $20, it will probably rise from that level because many traders are likely to buy it at support levels. After finding out a potential support level, traders try to spot the nearby resistance level where the rising price is expected to pause. Suppose a technical level is appearing at $60. So, the trader can buy at $20 and exit when the price reaches $60. If everything goes right, he can risk $20 to reap a reward of $60. In this trade, the risk-reward ratio will be 1:3.

By calculating the risk-reward ratio, traders can plan how much money they will need to invest, and how much reward they can expect to gain from any trade. This makes them cautious about money management and risk management.

Some traders have a flexible risk-reward ratio for trading, while others prefer to take trades only with a fixed risk-reward ratio. Keeping stop-loss in all trades also helps in managing the risk-reward ratio. Traders can calculate their trade entry point to stop-loss as the risk, and trade entry to profit as the reward. This way, they can find out if any trade has a bigger risk than the potential reward or a bigger reward than the potential risk. Choosing trades with bigger profits and smaller risks can increase the amount of profit over a period.

Without learning money management, all your knowledge about stock and day trading is useless. If you don't use effective techniques for managing your investment, then you may soon find your money running out and you will have to shut down your day trading business. There are various methods for money management in intraday trading. It will be a good idea to learn a few techniques for it and it and strictly apply those rules to your trading business. Keeping the trading cost to a minimum and putting stop-loss in all trades are effective money management tricks.

Margin trading facilities are given for day trading and can be used astutely for increasing profits. At the same time, margin facilities can make day traders greedy, make them commit the mistake of over-trading, and incurring losses. Margin facility is borrowing money from your brokerage firm and trading on borrowed money is never a good idea. It is better to avoid margin trading until you have enough experience in stock markets and can handle your emotions while trading.

Day trading is not only profitable but can always lead to losses because of the ever-present market risk. Various events can trigger this risk and affect the performance of the overall stock markets. Day traders have no control over it. However, many strategies can help day traders avoid market risk, and reduce the potential loss that it can cause. Knowledge of stock markets' functioning and checking economic calendars can help day traders avoid some market risks.

Traders always face the risk of financial loss. Therefore, they must use strategies for risk management in day trading. Protecting your trading capital should be your first aim so you can stay in the day trading business for the long term. Creating trading plans and trading strategies are steps that can help traders avoid loss-making trades. Using stop orders is another method that can help traders reduce the losses and book their profits at the right time.

Calculating the risk-reward ratio is another method for money management and reducing risk trading. Traders can calculate how much risk a trade carries and how much potential profit it can earn for them. They can choose only those trades that carry a bigger reward and smaller risk and thus earn more profits in the long-term. Some professional traders prefer to trade only when the rewards are much higher than the potential risk.

CHAPTER 13
Money Management

What is Money Management?

Money management is not a new aspect of the financial management world. It started when there was a rise of capitalism. When the economy was under a system that was dominated by private owners, they had their private properties and gained on the profits. Money Management started in around 1600, and individuals only survive by depending on how effectively they get their income. In the present age, to be successful financially involves having the ability and the zeal to save more, and lean on investing any surplus.

Money management is a term to refer to the many ways people manage their financial resources. It ranges from budget planning in regards to their income. Money management involves planning and purchasing items that are important to you. Without planning well and lack of money management skills, the amount a person has will always not be enough for them.

Before anyone starts on the money management journey, you need to be aware of the assets and liabilities that you have. Some of the examples of Personal assets and properties are cars, home, retirement, investment, and bank accounts. On the other hand, personal liabilities are loans, debts, and mortgages. To be able to know your net worth, you should see the difference between your assets and liabilities. When the liabilities are higher than the assets, then you have a lower net worth. Having excellent money management skills, you will be able to avoid this.

Goal setting helps in Money management. Without goal setting, you will be worried about daily bill management; this can adversely affect your long term goals. With goal setting, you can have a clear view of the expenses needed to, and which needs to be cut out. A perfect example is when you have a goal of getting a car worth $30,000, your goals will be to cut down your expenses. Similar to someone whose goals are to get a $20,000 car?

After planning and knowing your goals, start creating your budget. A budget is an estimation of income for a defined period of time — a tool which will assist you in managing your money well. With a budget, you will be able to save some cash and be able to minimize impulse buying. An example of a reasonable budget will be to allocate $250 for entertainment and miscellaneous expenses a month after settling the basic needs. If your income increases, it would be advisable to add the extra income to your savings plan and not adding it to the expenses budget.

When budgeting, you will have multiple accounts to manage. For example, you may have an emergency fund and saving accounts. By doing this, you will avoid the temptations of spending the funds on impulse buying. The retirement plan should be kept separate from the other accounts. There are different software that you can use to assist you in money management. An example of a money management software is Quicken; it helps in tracking your various accounts and ensuring your saving and spending goals are on the right track.

The different aspects of money management include analyzing, planning, and executing a financial portfolio. The financial portfolio includes investment types, taxes, savings, and banking. In business management, there are economic variables that might affect your business finances. The best Money Management skills are to be able to access and control all the factors that might affect your financial position.

You can achieve your set goals through excellent money management. A dream of owning a home without using student loans, and be able to have a stress-free life from debts. Have a better plan to be able to deal with unpredictable events that can affect your finances; like loss of employment, serious illness. With Money Management, you will be able to have some savings that will cover your unexpected events.

Internet is a global computer network that contains information and provides communication. Banking, investment, and insurance needs did not exist before. In the past days, customers had restrictions on decisions making in their financial matters, with less information on their options in their local areas. With the lack of internet connection, there was limitation and restrictions on where to find the right information. People had to go shopping for different items, like furniture and electronics. And also the purchasing of mortgages and insurance policies.

Money Management Skills

Do you know your income expenditure? Do you know your shopping, clothing and entertainment expenses?

Money Management is a life skill which is not in the school curriculum. Most people learn it from our parents on how to handle money. Since most people didn't learn about financial skills in school, you can still learn them now. Here are some of the Money management skills that you can follow to improve your skills.

Set a Budget

Track how you spend your money. Do you spend on food, movies, entertainment, and clothes? Do you frequently have an overdraw of your bank account? If this is true, then set a budget. Check your bank statements and note down how much is your expenditure categorically. You will find out how much wastage of money you are not aware of.

Spend wisely

Have a shopping list when you go to the grocery store? Do you first check the price of an item before putting the item in your basket? Use coupons if available. Use online resources and mobile apps to stay focused on your expenditure.

Monitor your spending! By not being attentive to these small tips, you will keep on losing money. It takes time to get coupons, and It takes some effort to find coupons and writing a shopping list and checking the price of an item before buying, it will all be worth it in the long run.

Balance your books

Most people rely on going online to look at their bank balance. By doing this, you won't be able to know how much you are spending at the moment. The best advice is to be accountable by recording all your expenses; you will have avoided over-spending.

Set a plan

You must have a plan for you to accomplish anything. For you to go from location A to B, it won't be possible without a GPS to show the routes. You will end up driving aimlessly going nowhere.

This is similar to not having a financial plan. You will always be broke and not knowing where your money is spent on. "Where did that money go?" With a great plan, you will be able to track your money and expenditure.

Think like an investor

The education system does not teach about handling money, mainly how to invest in growing your wealth. The rich people did not just save $500 a month; they learned how to grow their savings and invest. Turning that $500 into $1000, then into $10,000 and eventually into $100,000 and more.

By investing and growing your money, you will have secured a stable financial future. Think like an investor, and see your money grow.

Have the same financial goals with your partner/spouse

If you're married and you have a joint bank account, then learn to work together. You must both agree with the financial goals.

Make a budget and also see a financial adviser to learn how to invest your money. You must ensure that you have the same financial goals and stay focused.

Save Money

Have a strong commitment to saving your money and securing your future. You can improve your financial situation and make it better! But you need to start with the decision to do so. Make a decision to start saving your money and improving your management skills.

Importance of Money Management

Sticking to a budget and living within your means — is proper money management. Look for great price bargains and avoiding bad deals when purchasing. When you start earning more money, understanding how to invest will become an essential way of reaching your goals like having down payment for a home. Understanding the importance of excellent money management will help you achieve your plans and future goals. Some of the importance of Money Management are:

Better Financial Security

Being cautious of your expenditures and saving, you will be able to save enough for the future. Saving will give you financial security to deal with any unexpected expenses or emergencies like loss of employment, your car breaking down or even saving for a holiday. Having savings, you will not have to use a Credit card to settle crises. Saving is a crucial part of money employment as it helps you build your financial security for a secured future.

Take Advantage of Opportunities

You may encounter opportunities to invest in a business to make more money or an exciting experience like a good deal on a holiday vacation. A friend may inform you of a great investment opportunity or get a great once-in-a-lifetime dream holiday vacation. It can be frustrating not having the money to jump right to these opportunities.

Pay Lower Interest Rates

With excellent money management skills, you can determine your credit score. The highest score means you pay your bills on time and with low-level total debt. Having a higher credit score, you can save more of what you have and have a lower interest rate for car loans, mortgages, credit cards, and even car insurance. And there is the chance to brag to your friends about your high credit score at the parties.

Reduce Stress and Conflict

Paying your bills on time can have a relieving feeling. But on the other hand, being late in paying your bills cause stress and have a negative impact like shutdown in your gas and water supply. Always being broke before your next paycheck can bring conflict and, a significant amount of stress for, couple. And, as we all know, stress brings health problems, experts say, like hypertension, insomnia, and migraines. Being aware of how you can manage your finances, so you have extra cash and savings can put your mind at ease. You will enjoy a stress-free life.

Earn More Money

With your income growing, your financial planning will not only include budgeting for monthly expenses but also figuring out where to invest the extra cash that has accumulated. Knowing different kinds of investments for example stocks and mutual funds, you can earn more money from the investments than what you could have made by leaving the money in your savings account in your bank. But be aware not all investments are recognized as a good investment idea, for example, offshore casinos. One of the best benefits of having investments, you can be at work earning monthly income, and your investments, on the other hand, are making more money for you.

More saving and time

Excellent money management can assist in avoiding your finances from spiraling out of control. It is easy to be in debt if you are unaware of how all your income it's spent monthly. Effective money management means better use of your spare time. You can spend time with your family and friends, by having a clear budget, you will be able to plan for fun days out as you will have available cash to do so. Peace of mind

Excellent money management gives you some level of calm and peace of mind. With your income and the savings, you can handle any financial demands with the confidence that you have the resources to handle any need that will arise.

Best Money Managers

When developing your investment strategy, you will find yourself seeking some assistance. A well-chosen money manager can help you achieve your financial goals. Research is vital, find the right money manager who will be the perfect fit for your financial goals. There is a lot of information you can get to be able to find a money manager. You can rely on referrals, the internet, or financial companies to get the right money manager for you. In this segment we will go through what a money manager is. How does it work? What is the difference between a money manager and a financial advisor? What is the role of a money manager? What are the pros and cons of having a money manager? And what are the fees required?

Who is a Money Manager?

A money manager, also known as investment managers or portfolio managers. It's an individual or a firm which manages investments portfolio and provide personalized financial advice to an individual or institutional investor. Money managers offer advice to clients about the steps they should take to increase their returns.

How does it work?

Money managers earn a fee for their services and not a commission. In some cases, a client will pay a percentage of the managed assets to their money manager. In this way, both the client and the money manager will work hard towards the success of the portfolio. Here is an example illustrating how money managers work:

Suppose Mary has $20,000 and she wants to invest the money. She will find a money manager to manage her new portfolio. Then she schedules a meeting with the money manager. The money manager inquires about Mary's investment goals, the risk if the investment is a short-term or long-term, etc. Based on Mary's feedback, the money manager will choose a set of securities that will help Mary achieve her financial goals. The money manager will monitor Mary's portfolio on a monthly fee basis, the performance and the value of the portfolio.

What's the difference between a money manager and a financial advisor?

When it comes to your finances, doing it alone can be intimidating as you try to understand the game plan. You need to find the right professional to assist you in meeting your goals.

A financial advisor and a money manager have a lot in common, the two jobs are different, and they can't be handled by one person. A financial advisor is also known as wealth managers. A financial advisor understands the specifics of the client's economic life and creates a detailed investment plan, that is is also known to help the client meet their financial goals. A money manager focuses on managing the strategy your portfolio is invested in.

The role of a money manager:

A good money manager focuses on successfully managing your portfolio strategies, and should be able to meet the following expectations:

- To consistently manage investments portfolio with their stated investment objectives
- Appropriate risk management
- Avoid unnecessary turnover within the management team
- Operate transparently

What are the pros and cons of having a money manager?

When you have a financial goal, you want it to be a success. One of the ways to achieve that is by getting an expert to help you achieve your goals. Do you have some savings which you are thinking of investing? Then you need a money manager for you to achieve your goals of investing. You need a trustworthy and focused money manager. Consider a lot of things before hiring one. To be able to make the right choice, here are some of the pro and cons of having a money manager:

The pros:

Your money manager knows the financial environment

Your money manager can assist you in constructing an income statement and help you understand the market competition. With a great money manager, you can get an excellent customized financial plan and gain essential insights that will help you in your journey.

Your financial manager will make sure your money financial wisely

If there ever a time that you needed to make sure that your cash made the most significant impact, it's now. With a strained economy, there is no room for errors. Your money manager will assist you to avoid the risks and make sure your money it's spent in a way that will bring the best returns. Wondering whether to expand? If you are also thinking of increasing your investment, a money manager makes the smartest and best-informed decisions and assist you with any questions that you might have.

A money manager will free up your time to do what's most important

Your money manager will take away the stress of financial oversight, and this allows you to focus on other vital parts of life.

Your money manager can help your business function well

If you run a business, the money manager can help you with your business. To find out why invoices taking too long without getting paid, why your business is losing cash, and you are not sure where the wastage is happening. The money manager can implement control measures that allow you to easily track your money movement.

The cons:

Your money manager could be expensive

The main reason for not hiring a money manager is the cost! Your concern is a valid one. Money managers are highly qualified and experienced and usually request higher charges. Who can afford an expensive money manager when you have come a long way without him or her up to this point? The solution here is to do your research to get an affordable money manager who will give you the best quality results as well.

Performance Not Guaranteed

Although your money is managed professionally by the money manager, there are still no guarantees. In a bad market day, even the best money manager may lose money.

Lack of Control

You might not have the time or the knowledge to wisely invest your money; it will not be 100% comforting to some people to hand over control of their money to a stranger.

What is a Money Management Rule?

Investing doesn't necessarily need you to be an expert in the field. As a matter of fact, you don't need to be rich to begin investing. However, most people fail to manage their money because they don't know where to start. Here are some of the rules of money management to guide you through your journey:

Have a plan

How much are you planning to invest? When do you want to invest? When do you plan to exit? You can start from the end and determine how much money you need to invest. Plan for the future, towards financial freedom.

Time is money

The earlier you start investing, the better advantage you will have. Time is the biggest asset you have. For every time you invest include retirement savings too. There isn't anything that can make up for the effect of compound interest. If you end up losing money in the market, there is enough time for you to recover when you need it. For example, if you invest $1k for five years, you can make equal to $1.8k or $2k in 6 years, assuming the rate of return is the same. It amounts to a 10% difference if you invest one year later.

Do you sincerely think the 10% difference is worth falling off your investment? Never use the "it's too early to start investing" phrase as an excuse to keep your money under the mattress. It's much better to begin late than never.

It's emotional

We usually make most of our money decisions emotionally like greed, nervousness, and fear. To be able to focus on your long-term investment plan, do not check your account on a daily basis. There are regular fluctuations in the market and individual stocks. If to are making long-term investments, you don't need the stress of constant checking.

A lot of investors get fear after checking the media, and they end up buying or selling their investments at the wrong time. To avoid making such a mistake, be ready, and try to stay calm.

Financial Goals

Set short term and long term financial goals. Grow your goals and adjust them monthly. Correct your failures and enjoy the success.

Save Money

Saving for regular expenses like home maintenance and car expenses. It's advisable to save 5-1o percent of the net income. Save 3 to 6 months of your income to an emergency fund.

Financial Status

Set different expenses and include your debt payments too. Compare the amount of money coming in and what's going out. Know your debts and net income.

Set a Budget

Budget and closely monitor your spending plan.

Record Expenditure

Carefully monitor your money. You can note down and adjust appropriately.

Know the Difference Between Needs and Wants

To quickly know the difference, a need is something that is required for survival. For example, food, shelter, clothes, and water while a want is everything else. Wants to make life a little bit enjoyable. Put more fused on Needs first. And spend on the Wants only after you have taken care of your needs.

Use Credit Sensibly

Consider credit for planned purchases only. Take the amount that you can comfortably afford to purchase on credit. Credit payments shouldn't exceed 20% of net pay. Don't borrow from a creditor to settle debt to another creditor.

Settle your bills on time

Keep a higher credit score. Talk to your creditors in advance to explain your situation, if you won't be paying your bills on time.

Tips Used for Money Management

Money management is a delicate topic. For most individuals, it can be overwhelming and intimidating. You may have retirement savings, or not having enough emergency savings. Whatever your concern is, having a good handle of your finances is the best option. Here are some money management tips to get you started.

Manage Monthly Pay

Know your monthly income to better manage your money. Monthly budget, including rent or mortgage payments, gas bills, and other expenses like student loan payments, can be stressful to keep track of. However, making small changes can help you reduce your debts and expenses. Add extra into your monthly payments. Another advice is to increase payments over a year, or another option is to sign up for an automatic payment program. This will assist you to save time and money every month, as payments are deducted automatically from your savings account.

Track Your Spending Habits

Play detective with your finances. You will need to check the financial status by yourself. It might be overwhelming by limiting yourself to monthly expenses. Check out credit card statements, utilities bank account statements and also electronic payment records. Create a spreadsheet or use a pen and paper and track your expenses.

You can also categories your expenses. For example, labeling purchases as Needs wants savings and debts. You can be more detailed and categories like transport, food, and clothing. It all depends on an individual, how much weeds you want to get. After you have compiled everything in one list, get the total of every category to see how you spend. You will be shocked by the amount of money you spend on a particular expenditure.

Design a budget

When you track your spending, it will naturally lead to the next step: creating a budget. With the numbers you have from tracking your spending, you can now decide how much money you want to go into each item in your budget. You can also scale back some areas of your expenses that you discover you're overspending. You can write a budget as detailed as you like. Everybody's budget is different. Keep the budget relatively simple.

For proper budgeting, guideline uses the 50/30/20 rule — a strategy to help you divide and allocate your monthly income. The fifty percent will go towards fixed costs example, mortgage or rent, taxes, debt and car payments. The thirty percent will go towards spending, for example, vacation and eating out. And the 20% should go towards savings including emergency fund or investing. Regularly monitor your budget. It's better to start with a basic budget than not having a budget at all. Always save more than you're spending.

Set Financial Goals

Once you have attained your emergency savings account, you should work towards establishing financial goals. The financial goals can be short term goals such as holiday and long term goals such as saving for college, a house or a retirement plan. The mistakes most people make with their budget is they're short-sighted. Have a long term focus, have a five or ten-year plan. For example, it's easy to get money and buy that fancy car but, you can easily forget that you have a long term plan to have kids, and this can bring new expenses. Try to anticipate those long term goals and how to achieve them.

Set an Emergency Fund

You never know what the future will be. You could be unemployed or get an emergency. Whether you like it or not, life happens. Your emergency funding will be determined by your budget. Most financial expert's advice is saving 3 to 6 months' worth of expenses. Having an emergency fund to handle unplanned problem will help you feel more secured and prepared. Take away stressful emergencies with a financial cushion. Put your emergency fund in a savings account that is liquid and accessible, but only to be used for emergencies.

Apps Used for Money Management

Times are tough. Whether you earn a high net income or you get by, monitoring where your money is spent. There are many ways to track your spending, how you invest and more. We use our cell phones daily, and we always have our phones in our pockets all the time, using apps to help you manage your money is the best option.

Having a good understanding of your cash flow is very vital in managing your finances. How much of your income is coming in? When does the money get to your bank account? How do you spend the money? These are essential aspects of your financial success. Fortunately, there are a lot of money management apps in the market designed to help you check your bank balance, track your expenditure and, analyze your spending habits. Plus, there are apps that will assist you in making better financial decisions based on the data from your accounts.

And the best part? You can access your financial situation on the go. A lot of these money management apps can be checked online and also on your mobile device. It's very convenient as you can take care of your finances no matter where you are.

What do budget apps do? There are two main types of budget apps. One is an expense tracker — it best-fit people who deduct a lot of items from their taxes. For example, business owners who travel a lot, people who track their meals, transportation, and, all other professions who use expenses trackers. This app will help you track how much money you spend. You also have all the info you need when tax season rears its ugly head. The other type of budget app is the one which helps you track your bank budget, expenses bills, and utilities. These help you track your money, especially for people who manage multiple accounts and pays bills online.

Here are some of the best money management apps you should consider:

Personal Capital

Personal Capital has excellent features to track your budget and also include information about your investment accounts. And you can easily view on tablets, laptops, desktops and your mobile. It also shows graphs of your investments, that are easy to read and track down your investment performance.

Mint

Mint is one of the popular budgeting apps. Mint offer features like access to your investment accounts and budgeting tools. The budgeting portion is the main feature, and the investing part is little like an afterthought. The best app if you want to keep a very detailed budget. Mint also has a reminder feature to when your bills are due, and you can also pay your bills from the app.

Acorns

Acorns take virtual change out of your account. Instead of saving it, the app invests the difference. The app helps you start investing with virtually no effort. You can use Acorns on your transactions. The app has a new shopping type function, Found Money.

YNAB

YNAB is an acronym for You Need a Budget. YNAB cost $6.99 per month, but they waive the first month's fee. The philosophy for YNAB is " a job for every dollar." YNAB also offers a bank syncing and support feature. YNAB can also help you set your financial goals and make the most of each dollar earned.

Honeydue

Many couples use spreadsheets to manage their household finances. Honeydue is the best app for couples as it helps couples best co-manage their money. Honeydue helps to track shared bills; the pair can see their accounts in one spot, comment on the transactions, and build bigger and better financial goals. Honeydue has the main feature; couples can decide on how much they can share information with their significant others. This feature helps them to remain focused on their goals and not get caught in the weeds, arguing over the small stuff.

PocketGuard

PocketGuard will help you find savings in your spending. This app sync with your accounts and enables you to track and analyze your spending, which you can use that data to help you build an excellent budget. You can identify a pattern in your monthly spending, track your bills, and save some money.

Dollarbird

Dollarbird is an app that assists people who have issues with budgeting. This is a free app; however, it has premium add-ons. Your budget is put in a calendar form, and you can view any upcoming expenses. Other features are, you can color code transactions by category and pay you bills through the recurring transaction. Dollarbird lets you see the projected balance, so you are aware of how much money you can safely spend. The limitation that comes with this app is that the app does not sync with your bank account. With this app, you can quickly enter your transactions manually, and this means you will be more involved with the approach to your money.

Credit Karma

Credit Karma offers you access to your Credit Report. There are several uses of this app, for example, a company can use the app to determine whether to employ you or to estimate your credit score so as a business can be able to figure out the rates that they will charge you. This app can also be used to determine your loan applications and credit cards. Credit Karma is free to users however, the app earns money by offering targeted ads based on your credit score.

CONCLUSION

Thank for making it through to the end of this book. Successful day trading is a journey; it's not a destination. In this journey, you're going to change.

If you are new to the day trading business, this book will act as your guide. It will show you the map, the way of reaching your goal of becoming a successful trader. This book will tell you where to start, which steps to take in the journey of day trading, and finally, how to train yourself so that you can become a successful trader.

Please remember, you will not become a successful trader by just reading this book. You will have to practice the rope tricks this book shows you about day trading. When it comes to trading, our reaction to the market is more important than what happens in the markets.

Knowing is just half the battle. Action or applying what you learned is the other half of successful day trading. Without action, you have zero chances of becoming a successful day trader down the line. But if with it, you have a fighting chance.

You don't need to apply all that you've learned at once. Take baby steps, one at a time. The important thing is you start building momentum. The longer you put off action, the higher your risks are for failure.

Lightning Source UK Ltd.
Milton Keynes UK
UKHW051528261022
411061UK00020B/924